Burning Beethoven
Erik Kirschbaum

Burning Beethoven
The Eradication of German Culture
in the United States during World War I
By Erik Kirschbaum

Editor: Cindy Opitz

© 2014 by Berlinica Publishing LLC
255 West 43rd St., Suite 1012, New York, NY, 10036; USA
Print book ISBN
978-1-935902-85-0

E-book ISBN:
978-1-935902-86-7
978-1-935902-87-4
978-1-935902-88-1

LCCN: 2014933317

Cover photo: Historical Society of Madison, Wisconsin
Cover Design: Jennifer Durrant, Sue Yerou
Printed in the United States

www.berlinica.com

Sign up for our monthly newsletter at www.berlinica.com
and get a free e-book

Burning Beethoven

The Eradication of German Culture in the United States during World War I

Erik Kirschbaum

New York, 2015

Berlinica

ACKNOWLEDGEMENTS

THERE are many people who have altruistically helped me with this book and without their help this might not have ever been finished. Tom Heneghan, Dave Graham, Cora Lee Kluge, David Crossland, Yvonne Wagner, Michelle Martin, Steven Kirschbaum, Esther von Krosigk, Karin Scandella, Scott Reid, Deirdra Preis, Angelika Kirschbaum, Danae Grant, Dean Grant, and Ingrid Kirschbaum offered insightful and motivational ideas. Thanks also to Thomas Archdeacon of the University of Wisconsin for his guidance, as well as to Cornelius Sommer, William C. McDonald and Ulrich Müller of the American-German Studies Department.

Thanks also to Olaf Zapke, Noah Barkin, and Stephen Brown at Reuters for their support while I worked on this, and to Dr. Eva Schweitzer, Berlinica's publisher, for her ideas and guidance, and to Cindy Opitz, who did a splendid job editing the manuscript.

Contents

For Yvonne and Tom

DEDICATION

When Joseph Kirschbaum was growing up in a German section of New York City, he spoke just one language with his friends and family: German. There were bastions of ethnic Germans like his community in other towns and cities across the country. In Chicago, Milwaukee, Cincinnati, St. Louis, and many other places across America, there were neighborhoods and entire districts where German was the only language spoken.

It wasn't until Joseph Kirschbaum started attending school in 1896 that he began to learn English. But German remained his first language and first love until he was in his twenties, as it was for many millions of German-Americans at the turn of the Twentieth century. Although he never set foot outside of the United States, he spoke German effortlessly and with great pleasure.

Many years and two world wars later, I asked Joseph Kirschbaum, my grandfather, for help with a high school German assignment. A frown spread across his face. "No," he snapped. And then, after a few moments of unaccustomed silence from the normally affable man, he said: "I don't remember any of it."

This book is for Joseph Kirschbaum, who was either forced to forget or forced to deceive.

INTRODUCTION

Robert Paul Prager was a German immigrant trying to get a job in a coal mine near St. Louis in 1918 when he was lynched by a mob of Americans eager to show their patriotism and support of the World War I effort. They accused Prager of being a German spy and got away with killing the thirty-three-year-old immigrant without punishment. Prager was only one of more than thirty Germans killed in vigilante attacks in the United States during World War I, yet his hanging death epitomizes that dark and long-forgotten era of United States history, when anti-German hysteria swept across the country.

Prager, a short man with a handlebar mustache, was hanged from a tree by a mob on the outskirts of a small town in southern Illinois. The vigilantes who killed Prager were applauded in court and in many parts of the United States for "doing their part" to help fight the war over in Europe. The dozen men tried for his murder were acquitted just weeks later, at the end of a hasty trial during a period of intense patriotic fervor. During the twenty months when the United States was at war in Europe, others at home were killed, seriously hurt, or otherwise maltreated or punished by the justice system, convicted of sedition on trumped-up charges, or simply interned without charges or any justification other than that they were German aliens or German-Americans. They were often falsely accused of being spies, saboteurs, or were even assaulted or abused just for being German or of German origin. Many were even persecuted simply for expressing a critical opinion about the war, even though many mainstream Americans and members of other ethnic groups had also spoken out against U.S. participation in the war before 1917.

The midnight lynching of Prager by a bumbling band of amateur executioners was the most horrific of the attacks against German immigrants and still serves—a century later—as the most chilling illustration of wartime violence against German-Americans. It was a powerful and sudden eruption of virulence against what had, until then, been one of the country's biggest, proudest, and most successful ethnic groups. It was all the more surprising, considering how respected and well-established German culture had been in the United States prior to World War I. German-Americans were often leaders in engineering, science, medicine, music, and society. The widely admired German university system had been used as the archetype for many American universities, while the industriousness and work ethic of German immigrants had made an enduring impression. All of these positive contributions made it difficult to fathom the suddenness and intensity of anti-German sentiment that swelled during World War I, engulfing the country and all but wiping out what had, until then, been a thriving German-American culture.

Nearly a century later, another wave of patriotic fervor swept across the United States in the wake of the September 11, 2001, terrorist attacks that destroyed the World Trade Center and damaged the Pentagon. Enemies of the United States—whether real or perceived—were demonized. Especially Arab-Americans, who failed in the eyes of some to show enough support for the United States, were also treated as villains. Muslims in general—even Sikhs, who were apparently targeted just for wearing turbans—suffered under racist attacks and became victims of discrimination and random assaults. About five hundred hate crimes against Arab-Americans and Muslims were recorded in the months after the September 11, 2001, terrorist attacks.

This more recent, intense wave of American patriotism included even resentment against allied countries such as France and, again, Germany, for not showing enough support for the United

States' war in Iraq. French fries were renamed "Freedom fries" in American restaurants and the Congressional cafeteria, French restaurants were boycotted, French wine was poured into gutters, and American talk show hosts, pundits, and bloggers made racists jokes about the French, depicting them as "Cheese Eating Surrender Monkeys". In the eyes of patriotic Americans, there was no room for differentiation between someone holding a different point of view and someone committing treason, both in 1917–18 and in the years immediately after 2001.

Some people experienced a sense of déjà vu since eight decades earlier, in an even worse patriotically fueled onslaught against German names, sauerkraut was renamed "liberty cabbage" and German measles became "liberty measles." There are many eerie parallels between the anti-German sentiment that ripped through the United States a century ago and the anti-Arab and anti-Muslim sentiment of the last decade—as well as the anti-Japanese sentiment that gripped the United States after the 1941 attack on Pearl Harbor. Changing names to "liberty cabbage" or "freedom fries" might sound ridiculous now. But a century ago, when German culture itself was under attack, the eradication of German names was merely the tip of an iceberg.

In recent years, there have been efforts to repair, if only symbolically, some of that past damage to German-Americans. In one remarkable ceremony on May 3, 2006, in Montana's capital city of Helena, then-Governor Brian Schweitzer posthumously issued pardons to seventy-eight German-Americans who had been convicted on trumped-up charges of sedition during World War I. Among the crimes of those seventy-eight German-Americans was merely making critical comments about the war. Some were persecuted for not buying enough Liberty Bonds—war bonds sold in the United States to raise funds to support the Allied cause—or for criticizing wartime food regulations or refusing to publicly kiss the American flag. This was a popular way to test a person's patriotism at the time. Montana, where Germans comprised the biggest immigrant group, was one of twenty-seven states that passed a sedition law giving authorities sweeping powers to prosecute German-Americans. The Montana law was especially strict and made it a crime to say or publish anything "disloyal, profane, violent, scurrilous, contemptuous or abusive" about the American government, soldiers, or flag.

The Montana sedition law later served as a prototype for the National Sedition Act passed by Congress in 1918. The children of some of those sent to jail for sedition in Montana were taken away from their parents and given to other families in forced adoptions. Montana, like some other states, also went so far as to make it a crime to even speak German and banned books written in German. Schweitzer, a grandson of ethnic German immigrants from Russia and Ukraine who arrived in the United States in 1909, did not only posthumously pardoned those German-Americans convicted, but he also apologized to their families. "I'm going to say what Governor Sam Stewart should have said," Schweitzer began—a reference to the Montana governor who signed the sedition law in 1918. "I'm sorry, forgive me, and God bless America, because we can criticize our government," the governor said in an emotional speech. "In times when our country is pushed to our limits, those are the times when it is important to remember individual rights."

Burning Beethoven is about a time in America when civil liberties were trampled upon. It will shine a light on that brief and intense, yet largely overlooked and forgotten chapter of American history. It is an attempt to explain why the once so large, proud, and influential German-American ethnic minority surrendered so much of its cultural identity under pressure. It is based on research I began as a student at the University of Wisconsin in 1984 for my senior honor's thesis, *The Eradication of German Culture in the United States: 1917–18,* that was originally published within the series Deutsch-Amerikanische Studien at the Hans-Dieter Heinz Akademischer Verlag in Stuttgart.

Burning Beethoven is an expanded and updated examination of that harrowing episode of American history and includes a deeper exploration about the wartime assault on German culture and how that sinister period compares with the modern-day excesses that were seen once again in the United States after the terror attacks of 9/11.

The title, *Burning Beethoven*, serves as a metaphor to describe in broad terms the furor, the rage, and the attacks that blindsided Germans, German-Americans, their culture, their literature, their language, and their music. Beyond the mob-killings of some German-Americans and German aliens, German-language books, magazines, and newspapers were set on fire in public burnings and German-language instruction stopped in a number of states; the music of German composers, including Beethoven, was banned in some cities, and ordinary German immigrants were arrested and locked up in detention camps, sometimes for years, simply because they were German and were somehow considered a threat to the security of the United States.

Today there are about fifty million Americans who more or less proudly trace their origins to Germany, the 2010 census found. That makes German-Americans the largest ethnic group in the United States—larger than the Irish-American, African-American, and Anglo-American group. But precious few speak German or have any ties to the country of their ancestors. No other country in the world took in more German immigrants than the United States. Those fifty million Americans of German ancestry comprise about one-third of the world's German Diaspora. But where did they go in the United States and what happened to them? Why were the ties between America's largest ethnic group and the European homeland severed so completely? *Burning Beethoven* will try to answer those questions about the eradication of German culture in United States during World War I.

This bed-and-breakfast in Fredericksburg, Texas, established in 1915, managed to survive the anti-German hysteria during World War I.

Chapter 1

The Lynching of Robert Paul Prager

Robert Paul Prager was nineteen years old when he left his home in Dresden, Germany, for what he hoped would be a better life in the United States. He joined millions of immigrants from Germany and other parts of Europe who sailed across the Atlantic in search of prosperity and the pursuit of happiness. Single and uneducated, like many of his contemporaries, Prager arrived in the United States in 1905 and drifted for years, laboring in unskilled jobs throughout the Midwest. He ended up getting into trouble with the law in 1912, while living in Gary, Indiana, and spent a year in jail for theft.

Like other German aliens in the United States, Prager had been complacent about obtaining American citizenship. Even after 1914, when World War I broke out in Europe, Prager felt no urgent need to become a U.S. citizen because the United States was a neutral nation, and the powerful German-American community mounted a campaign to keep the United States out of the war.

But that was changing. The first major shift in sentiment followed the sinking of the *Lusitania*, a British ocean liner by a German submarine in May 1915. There were 128 Americans among the 1,198 passengers and crew that perished. Now, America began to drift slowly toward joining Britain and France in the war against Germany. But only in early 1917 would America join the battlefields in Europe, after British spies intercepted a secret telegram from Germany's deputy foreign minister, Arthur Zimmermann, to Mexico. In the telegram, Zimmermann recklessly attempted to persuade Mexico to invade the United States. The United States declared war on Germany just a few weeks later. Only then, Prager frantically tried to become an American citizen. But since his adopted homeland was now at war with his native country, it was too late.

Caught up in the patriotic fervor that was sweeping the nation, Prager tried to join the U.S. Navy. But he was half blind and had a glass eye, and his application was rejected. He moved to St. Louis, and eventually ended up in Collinsville, Illinois, a small town of about four thousand, just a few miles northeast of St. Louis. Prager worked as a baker there for several months, while trying to join a coal miners' union. While his application to the United Mine Workers union was pending, Prager was allowed to work in a coal mine in nearby Maryville.

In early April 1918, at a point when a German army offensive was achieving unexpected successes against the Allies on the battlefields in Europe, dashing American hopes for a quick end to the war and fueling anti-German sentiment, Prager's application for union membership was formally denied.

"As a German alien, Prager was suspect," noted Frederick Luebke in his 1974 book, *Bonds of Loyalty.* "A stranger, unmarried, stubbornly argumentative, given to Socialist doctrines, blind in one eye, he looked like a spy to the miners of Maryville. Actually, a less likely candidate for espionage could hardly be found, but these miners were not inclined to rational analysis." Angered by what he believed to be an injustice, Prager wrote an embittered appeal directly to the miners, urging them to overrule their bosses and accept him into their union. He posted carbon copies of his appeal, which was critical of union leaders, around town on what would be the final day of his life.

After reading the statement that Prager had posted, a group of miners gathered in a saloon to discuss the German alien stirring up trouble in their community. In light of the discouraging news from Europe about the course of the war and the accompanying rise of patriotism roiling the United States, they saw Prager's appeal to overrule their union leaders as a call for anarchy. They decided to take matters into their own hands and defend the country against what they saw as a dangerous German anarchist.

Fueled in part by their after-work alcohol consumption, the miners went to the boarding house where Prager was living, at about 9:30 p.m. They told him to leave town within ten minutes. Prager was scared and agreed to leave, but he tried to convince the miners that he had as much American patriotism as they did. "Brothers, I am a loyal USA workingman," he told them. Some of the miners seemed disappointed by Prager's ready compliance and decided to force him to strip down to his underclothes and parade down Main Street, wrapped in an American flag. He walked barefoot and sang the "Star-Spangled Banner."

Curious onlookers came out to see what was happening, and a crowd soon gathered. Police arrived and decided to take Prager into protective custody at the jail, but the crowd followed them. As it waited outside the police station, what was turning into a mob was at first indecisive and leaderless. Then the town's twenty-eight-year-old mayor, Dr. John Siegel, arrived. The mayor tried to persuade the crowd to leave, pleading with the increasingly rowdy gathering to go home, saying that federal authorities would handle the matter in the morning and that Prager deserved the chance of a fair trial. "We do not want a stigma marking Collinsville," Mayor Siegel said, according to a news report in the *St. Louis Globe Democrat* on April 5. "And I implore you to go to your homes and discontinue this demonstration."

At about the same time, one of the town's police officers tried to trick the mob into believing that Prager had been taken away from the jail by driving a car away from the building from a dark alley at high speed. But the officer returned the car to the police station only a few minutes later, just as the mob was starting to break up. No one was fooled, and the mob was reinvigorated by the unexpected turn of events and quickly reassembled in front of the jail.

Mayor Siegel then ordered all saloons in the town to close for the night, erroneously believing that might calm the situation down. But closing the taverns only had the opposite effect, galvanizing the locals eager to prove their patriotism. The police officer who delivered the mayor's shutdown order to the saloons also unwittingly added to the excitement in Collinsville that evening by bringing news that a genuine "German spy" had been captured.

After the saloons were closed, the mob in front of the jail swelled from about seventy-five to several hundred. They demanded that they be allowed to search the jail themselves. The mayor relented and agreed to allow one man, a respected and recently discharged veteran named Joseph Riegel, to go inside and inspect the jail on behalf of the crowd. But as soon as the door was opened to allow Riegel in, the mob poured in behind him.

At first the search of the jailhouse proved futile, but the mob eventually found Prager hiding in the basement. He was dragged outside and paraded to the outskirts of town. The police did not intervene to break up the procession, although they later claimed in court that they would have stepped in if it had it become apparent that Prager's life was in danger. The parade continued beyond the town limits, where the Collinsville police turned back because, as they later said, their authority did not extend any farther.

The march continued for about two miles outside the town. The idea was, as several members of the mob later testified, to tar and feather Prager—a common but painful method of "treating" Germans or other alleged "spies" caught in the United States during that time. But the mob was unable to find any hot tar, so they began trying to extract "confessions" from Prager about what they suspected was a German plot to sabotage the coal mine in Maryville. They demanded that he tell them the "truth" about his activities as a spy, about rumors that he hoarded gun-powder, and about questions he had allegedly asked about how much gun powder it would take to blow up a mine.

"Prager begged for mercy," according to the *St. Louis Globe-Democrat* report. "He said that he was a loyal citizen, and in a signed statement, which he had previously made to the police, he said that his heart and soul were for the United States." Amid confusion in the crowd, someone held up a rope, and a boy was sent up into a nearby tree to throw the rope over a limb. The mob put the rope around Prager's neck. Riegel then tried to pull the rope, but was unable to hoist Prager off the ground on his own. The former soldier then shouted, according to testimony heard later in court, "Come on fellows, we're all in this, let's not have any slackers here." As many as fifteen people then grabbed the rope to help Riegel, and Prager was hoisted into the midnight air.

"But these were amateur assassins," noted Luebke in *Bonds of Loyalty*. "They had neglected to tie their victim's hands." Prager tugged at the rope around his throat. Then a voice from the mob shouted, "Let him down! Let him say something if he wants to." Prager was lowered back down, and allowed to write a final letter. "Dear Parents," he wrote in German, "I must on this Fourth Day of April, 1918, die. Please pray for me, my dear parents. This is my last letter and testament. Your dear son and brother, Robert Paul Prager."

He prayed aloud in German and again insisted he was not a German spy or plotting to blow up a mine. He then told his executioners to go ahead and kill him if they must. But he also made a last request: "Wrap me in the flag when you bury me." He was hanged at 12:30 a.m. on Friday, April 5, 1918.

Most of the United States quickly learned of the Prager hanging. "This is the first killing for disloyalty in the United States, although many persons have been mobbed and tarred and feathered," wrote the *St. Louis Globe-Democrat*. And although many Americans and also newspapers condemned the mob violence, many others showed their support for the vigilantes. These felt that President Woodrow Wilson and Congress were not doing enough to fight disloyalty in the country, which had been deeply divided about the war long before the United States got into it. *The New York Times* and other newspapers denounced the mob's action and urged in editorials that a prompt trial and imprisonment of the leaders of the crime would be the only way to "vindicate the name of America."

But there were other newspapers, such as *The Chicago Herald* and *The Milwaukee Journal*, which wrote that they could understand why the mob had hanged Prager. *The Chicago Herald*, for example, seemed more concerned that Germany might retaliate against American prisoners of war. *The Milwaukee Journal* wrote in an editorial that unless Americans of German ancestry started displaying their loyalty to the United States more clearly, such actions by ordinary citizens against German-Americans were to be expected. On April 12, *The Washington Post* wrote that "in spite of excesses such as lynching, it is a healthful and wholesome awakening in the interior of the country." The *Edwardsville Intelligencer*, a local newspaper in southern Illinois, at first condemned the hanging, calling it "an unlawful and unjustifiable act." But the same newspaper printed that "it is a fact that we are at war with Germany and that no one in Germany could say or do things that are said and done here every day and live. A traitor over there is dealt with summarily."

There probably should not have ever been any doubt about Prager's loyalty, according to historian Donald Hickey. In an article on the "Prager Affair" in the *Journal of the Illinois State Historical Society* in 1969, Hickey wrote, "Prager was, in fact, as loyal to the United States as any native-born citizen, and his innocence was attested to by many who knew him. The night captain of the Collinsville Police and the superintendent of the mine at Maryville both asserted that there was no truth to the charge that Prager had hoarded powder. Two of the men with whom he boarded attested to Prager's loyalty . . . and a reporter found two American flags in his room."

Three weeks after the killing, twelve men were indicted for the lynching and put on trial. Despite the best attempts of Judge Louis Bernreuter to ensure a fair trial, he was unable "to rid the trial of its circus atmosphere," Hickey wrote. The defense centered its case around the notion that the war had created a "new unwritten law," in which a form of popular justice, that is to say mob rule, could be enforced by ordinary Americas who sought to protect themselves from disloyal citizens. The defense attorney had argued persuasively in his closing statement that this "unwritten law" justified the mob's lynching, and that it had been a "patriotic murder" because Prager had been a German spy. Judge

Bernreuter repeatedly instructed the jury, and the defense, that the war situation and Prager's loyalty were not in question at the trial, and that the only matter the jury had to decide was whether or not Prager had been hanged by the defendants.

On May 13, the jury found all twelve men innocent. It took the jury just forty-five minutes to reach its verdict—some of the newspaper accounts about the trial's conclusion said the jurors actually only took twenty-five minutes to come to their decision. The jury's not-guilty ruling was based on the fact that Prager had been murdered in a dark place and positive identification of the members of the mob was not possible. Another reason cited by the jurors for acquittal was the fact that there was contradictory testimony on who pulled the rope.

"Well, I guess nobody can say we aren't loyal now," shouted one of the jury members, a local farmer, after the trial ended. Many of the jurors wore red-white-and-blue ribbons to display their patriotism. "We've done justice of the right sort for Madison County," the farmer added, according to John A. Hawgood in his 1940 book, *The Tragedy of German America: The Germans in the United States of America During the Nineteenth Century—and After.*

J. O. Monroe, publisher of the local *Collinsville Herald*, wrote in an editorial after the trial, "Outside a few persons who may still harbor Germanic inclinations, the whole city is glad that the . . . men indicted for the hanging of Robert Prager were acquitted. The community is convinced that he was disloyal. The city does not miss him. The lesson of his death has had a wholesome effect on the Germanists of Collinsville and the rest of the nation."

Prager's murder in 1918 was only the most extreme example of hostility toward all things German in the United States, a reflection of the enmity that erupted after America entered World War I. It followed three tense years in which President Wilson and his government struggled to keep the United States neutral and out of the war, before finally joining the fight on the side of the Allies in 1917.

Wilson was motivated by idealism. But he had also been eager to win reelection in 1916, and keeping the United States out of the war had been a popular stance in many parts of the country, especially in states with large populations of German immigrants. German-Americans were generally proud of their heritage and their mother country, and, before 1917, they unabashedly used their influence to try to keep the United States out of the war. In a cabinet meeting on April 6, 1918, President Woodrow Wilson discussed the Prager hanging in Illinois. But he spurned the advice of Attorney General Thomas Gregory to issue a statement to calm the "nation and publicly condemn mob violence," according to Hans P. Vought in *The Bully Pulpit and the Melting Pot: American Presidents and the Immigrant, 1897–1933*. Wilson did not publicly talk about the Prager hanging until July 26—more than three months later—and then only indirectly. The president's failure to denounce the violence may have sent a tacit signal, opening the door for further attacks. In the following weeks, as anti-German fears rose amid the success of Germany's spring offensive in Europe, scores of incidents of tarring and feathering were reported, as well as near hangings of several German immigrants.

The case of Henry Rheimer was typical of the violence that erupted in the United States after Prager's murder. The fifty-year-old Rheimer was nearly hanged to death in Collinsville, Oklahoma, by a mob of about fifty men on the night of April 19, 1918—just two weeks after Prager was killed. Rheimer, who claimed he was of Russian and not German origin, was accused of disloyalty by a local branch of the Defense Council—a zealous patriotic organization that specialized in twentieth-century-style witch hunts. The Defense Council claimed it had "evidence" that Rheimer was a German and had accused him several months earlier of making unpatriotic remarks. The Defense Council had ordered him to fly an American flag in front of his house for the duration of the war. But Rheimer had taken the flag down earlier, on April 19, for which he was imprisoned. Later that night, a mob stormed into the jail, pushed its way past two patrolmen and the assistant police chief, and dragged Rheimer from his cell to the town hall.

There, according to a report in *The New York Times* on April 20,

"They wrapped a double electric light cord twice around his neck, attached the other end to the supports of a basketball [backboard], and commanded him to kiss every star in the flag." Rheimer complied and then apologized for whatever disloyal statements he might have made. "Then the chair was removed. The body swung twice past the goal post."

Assistant Police Chief Charles Miller arrived at that point and pleaded with the mob to give Rheimer the chance of a fair trial the next morning. Rheimer was unconscious but still alive when he was lowered down. He was taken to Tulsa, where he was placed in jail. At his hearing the next day, Rheimer testified that he believed that his neighbors "had it in for me" because his son had claimed exemption from the draft for religious reasons, and had been assigned to a job in the sanitation department instead of military duty.

Many similar stories of assault against German immigrants can be found in American newspapers and magazines from 1917 and 1918. The examples of Prager and Rheimer are unquestionably among the most disturbing illustrations of the malevolence that swept the country. The idea of American citizens "doing their part" to help the war effort in Europe and taking justice into their own hands by hanging suspected traitors was a concept that was even openly encouraged in many periodicals.

In light of violent outbursts of vigilantism like those seen in the Prager and Rheimer incidents, it is easy to understand why German immigrants abandoned their language and culture during World War I and helps explain why German culture, so fondly espoused by millions of immigrants at the turn of the century, disappeared so quickly and completely during the war.

A REMEDY FOR THE SOAP- BOX TRAITOR: *One of many cartoons published by* Life *magazine November 1, 1917 issue to tacitly endorse lynching German-Americans while depicting them as traitors.*

CHAPTER 2

ON A MISSION TO SPREAD GERMAN KULTUR

It is difficult to fully appreciate how large and influential the German-American population was in America at the turn of the nineteenth century. German immigrants played leading roles in fields ranging from engineering to science, medicine, literature, and music. Germans have been moving to the New World since 1683, first settling in Germantown, Pennsylvania, and New York. Millions more immigrated during the nineteenth century, attracted by the prospects of prosperity or political or religious freedom. Their manpower and skills helped the United States grow from a small rural country at the start of the nineteenth century into a bustling, prosperous nation on the verge of becoming one of the world's leading industrial nations by the end the century. Many immigrants from German-speaking parts of Europe in the earlier waves were farmers who settled in states such as Pennsylvania, New York, and Maryland. Many of those who came in the latter half of the nineteenth century settled either farther west in the Midwest farming regions or in urban areas and, before long, formed the dominant ethnic group in entire quarters of many towns and cities. In 1900, there were about eight million Americans of German ancestry in the United States, when the total U.S. population was seventy-six million, making German-Americans one of the largest ethnic groups at the time.

One century ago, German influence in the United States was more dominant than Hispanic influence is now. The first Bible ever printed in the United States, for example, was in German, in 1743.

In some parts of the country, German influence was so universal that non-German settlers—Irish and freed slaves, for example—ended up learning to speak German in order to communicate with other residents in their towns.

The English social historian John A. Hawgood observed the phenomenon in his 1940 book *The Tragedy of German-America*. Hawgood was intrigued by the fate of German culture in the United States as he saw it in the town of Belleville, Illinois, near St. Louis. Prior to World War I, Belleville had been an almost completely Germanic town, with a German-speaking mayor and a German-speaking majority on the city council. Three of the city's five newspapers were also written in German. In 1870, about ninety percent of the town's population was either German-born or of German ancestry. Belleville seemed to be the epitome, in Hawgood's eyes, of the hundreds of similar small bastions of Germania in America.

Belleville was by no means an isolated example of German culture flourishing in the United States before World War I. Many areas in the Midwest were filled with immigrants from German-speaking countries in Europe. Texas, Missouri, Pennsylvania, Ohio, and Wisconsin were states that became the new home for German settlers during the waves of nineteenth-century immigration. Seven counties in Pennsylvania were nearly entirely German, and large swaths of twenty-one other counties in the state were thoroughly German until the early twentieth century. This German outpost in Pennsylvania was so large and so influential, according to Heinz Kloss in *Language Loyalty in the United States*, that no special efforts were needed to preserve the German language there. On the contrary, he pointed out, "in order to bring about a change, special language-riddance efforts would have been needed." World War I proved to be an effective language-riddance tool.

There were especially high concentrations of German immigrants in Cincinnati, Milwaukee, and St. Louis—a region that was sometimes referred to as the "German triangle" or "German belt." In 1890, seventy percent of Milwaukee's residents were German or had German ancestry, while sixty percent of St. Louis's citizens were of German origin.

New York today: Remnants of a vibrant German-American past.
Above: The Astor family founded a free library in 1854 at W 20th St.
Below: The old house of the Deutsch-Amerikanische
Schützengesellschaft, the Rifle Society, at St. Mark's Place.

Texas, an independent republic until 1845, was also a popular destination for German immigrants. Some three million Texans have German ancestors, according to a recent census. Other regions where many Germans settled were Missouri and Wisconsin, which had become states in 1821 and 1848, respectively. In the years following 1848, when a revolution in European German-speaking principalities seeking a constitution and political freedoms failed, both Missouri and Wisconsin became destinations for hundreds of thousands of German immigrants.

Germans settling in Missouri founded many small communities along the Mississippi River north of St. Louis. Before World War I, the German language was used not only in the churches there, but on the streets, in schools, and in newspapers as well. Seventy percent of the Lutheran churches in St. Louis, for example, still had sermons delivered in German until 1914, and only one professor of eight in universities lectured in English. By 1929, those numbers would dwindle to twenty-five percent offering German sermons and just one professor lecturing in German.

In the half century before 1917, a higher number of German-speaking immigrants—more than three million—arrived in the U.S. than in any other comparable period. But the years between 1832 and 1860 also saw a high and steady flow of German-speakers coming into the United States. What is significant about these dates is that they may help explain why the Germans living in the U.S. ended up clinging to the culture and traditions they brought with them. It was a period of tremendous pride about German culture in German-speaking Europe. Johann Wolfgang von Goethe, the famous German poet, died in 1832, the year that marked the beginning of the era of greater emigration to the United States.

Ludwig van Beethoven, who died in 1827, might also have been on the minds or in the hearts of some immigrants from Central Europe upon arrival in the New World. Some even harbored a somewhat haughty belief that they were on a "mission" to spread a superior German culture across North America and were thus determined to retain their language and culture.

Their arrogance ran into a powerful enemy in the 1850s, the

so-called Nativist movement that also was fueled by antagonism directed against immigrants from other countries. Nativists were generally Americans of English origin. Aimed at the Irish ethnic communities as well as at the German immigrants, the Nativist movement turned out to be a harbinger of the persecution to follow seven decades later in 1917 and 1918. The Nativist movement led to the founding of the Know-Nothing party. The Know-Nothings of the mid-1850s wanted to place tight restrictions on immigration to limit the influence of Irish Catholics and German immigrants, a lot of whom also were Catholics. The movement was fueled by popular fears that the country was being overwhelmed by immigration, but after some modest successes in regional elections—the Know-Nothings also had a presidential candidate in 1852 and 1856—the party fell apart over differences on the slavery question that split the nation in the years leading up to the Civil War. Then, it largely disappeared.

It is worth noting that, prior to the anti-German sentiment stirred by the Nativist movement, Germans living in the U.S. had not been a united ethnic group at all. German immigrants had arrived in different waves and for a wide variety of reasons. Many of the first German-speaking settlers in the United States immigrated for religious reasons. Mennonites and even some Lutherans came in search of religious freedom and to avoid conscription in Germany, while the "Forty-Eighters" came after the 1848 revolution failed to achieve political reforms. There were many different religious groups scattered across a vast region east and west of the Mississippi. Aside from sharing the German language, many Germans had precious little in common, before the Nativist era changed that.

The Nativist threat was indeed a catalyst that forced a loose alliance among all of those diverse German groups, under the hyphen injected between the words "German" and "American." By creating a new word in the 1850s, the "German-Americans" were sending the message to their Anglo and Nativist tormentors that, even though they wanted to retain their German language and their fondness for their German culture, they were loyal to the United States. "Deutschland meine Mutter, Amerika meine Frau"

Fredericksburg, Texas: An antique kitchen cabinet at the local Pioneer Museum, with German-language sayings about the skills of housewives.

was an idea held by German-Americans that they could be "married" to America and yet still remain faithful to their "mother," or in other words, Germany. The idea that there is nothing wrong with having such dual loyalties has its roots in this period, according to Hawgood.

A further contributing factor to the Germans' ability to stave off the effects of assimilation at first was that many Germans who arrived in America sailed across the Atlantic as entire families, rather than as individuals. Compared with other ethnic groups, which were often largely made up of unattached individuals, the German immigrants tended to arrive even as extended families. The bonds to the nuclear family provided a basis for greater retention of their language and culture. Thus, coupled with an inclination by many Germans to settle in smaller, more rural areas, the effects of assimilation were retarded more for Germans than for other ethnic groups, Hawgood noted.

The predominance of Germans in the United States had considerable influence and also helped shape the language and traditions in America. In many parts of the country, but particularly in the Midwest, numerous German words and patterns of speech found their way into American English during this period. "Sauerkraut," "noodle," "dumb," "dummkopf," "and how" (from the German und wie), "standpoint," "shoe" (rather than the British term "boot"), "cookbook" (instead of "cookery-book"), "beergarten," "kindergarten," "gesundheit," "concertmaster," "iceberg," "rathskeller," "lied," "kaput," "hinterland," "plunder," "waltz," "Kris Kringle" (from a misunderstanding of the translation from German of Christkind), "wanderlust," "rucksack," "pretzel," "burger," "bub," "loafer" (from Landlaufer), "zig-zag," and "zwieback" are just a few of the myriad examples of German words imported directly into the English language, according to journalist and author H. L. Mencken in his 1919 book *The American Language.* Mencken had been sympathetic to Germans before and after World War I, and critical of British propaganda. The many German words that entered the American form of the English language are an indication of how deeply imbedded

German culture was becoming in the United States. The more sedate and reflective Christmas celebrations in America nowadays came about in part thanks to the influence of German immigrants who, with their imported tradition of Christmas trees, Santa Claus, and Kris Kringle, helped transform the holiday into more of a family celebration than had previously been the case. After the Revolutionary War, Christmas was considered an English tradition and fell out of favor for a time. Before the influx of Germans in the nineteenth century, Americans viewed Christmas as more of a rowdy occasion, and celebrations sometimes degenerated into whiskey-drinking sessions and brawls.

Up until 1882, German immigration into the United States continued to grow. In 1882 alone, there were 250,000 Germans who entered the United States, which was the all-time high. German immigration fell after 1882, however, and there was an even more precipitous decline after 1892. The slowing of German immigration also helped set the stage for the erosion of German culture in the United States. After 1892, German immigration into the United States never reached even 100,000 in any single year, and between 1895 and 1914, the annual average was just 30,000. This drop in numbers can partly be attributed to a newfound pride within Germany following the unification of the German Empire in 1871, engineered by the powerful and popular chancellor Otto von Bismarck, as well as to an economic boom in Germany, fueled by reparations paid by France after the Franco-German war.

But at the same time, Germans were at first discouraged from leaving Germany and then even blocked by the German government after 1888. In 1863 Bismarck issued an order to his Ministry of Commerce to discourage Germans from leaving, because, he said, "to emigrate was to betray the fatherland," according to Mack Walter in *Germany and the Emigration, 1816–1885*. While the order also slowed the flow of German immigration into America, the industrial boom which Germany experienced in the decades after its 1871 unification, combined with the rapid growth of the military, led to labor shortages in Germany, which were also factors that contributed to the precipitous slowing of German emigration.

Despite the falling numbers of new Germans arriving in the final two decades of the nineteenth century, the heavy flow in previous decades had helped German-Americans gain influence in many parts of American life. The German-language press was flourishing, reaching its zenith with a total of 894 German newspapers in 1894, according to Christine M. Totten's 1967 book *Roots in the Rhineland*. German-speaking theaters were also still popular in the United States at the time, German was spoken almost exclusively in churches and schools in many German-American communities, and German societies in America continued to enjoy large memberships and a high level of prestige.

Next to New York and Chicago, which was the world's sixth-largest German city in 1900, there were a myriad of small towns in America, particularly in the Midwest, where the German language was sometimes the only means of communication. Yet that would be the peak, and by the 1890s, there were already signs that the spread of German culture in the United States was waning. Not a single new German-language newspaper was founded in Texas after 1904, for example, and few German-language publications were launched anywhere after the turn of the century. This was a reversal of the trend in the previous decades, when new German-language publications were springing up all across the country. It was not so much a case of there being a sudden disdain of German that paved the way for the decline of the German press. Instead, the forces of assimilation were gradually eroding interest in German-language newspapers, as many German-born immigrants who had arrived earlier in the 1800s were dying away.

"Long before the war of 1914, cracks in the once solid structure of German-America had appeared," wrote historian John Hawgood. "And though efforts were made to paper over them, they widened rather than diminished during those placid pre-war days." Hawgood, who was surprised by the speed at which German culture in the United States disappeared during the war, pointed to the founding and rapid growth of the National German-American Alliance (NGAA), a federation of ethnic German associations established in 1901 by Charles J. Hexamer. He saw it

as one example of how some German-Americans were intentionally trying to maintain their culture as the younger generations became more American and less German. Also called the Deutsch-
amerikanische Nationalbund, its mission was to "promote and
preserve German culture in America." One of its aims was to
chronicle the important role that German-Americans played in
the development of the United States.

German-Americans did have reason to be proud of their ac-
complishments in turn-of-the-century America. Americans of
German ancestry had played a significant role in the growth and
development of the United States, which contributed to a growing sense of pride and belonging to a larger community. George
Westinghouse was one such prominent American of German descent. Among his many inventions was the train airbrake, a major safety breakthrough at the time. H. J. Heinz, who built the
world's first pickle factory, and Karl Steinmetz, whose numerous
discoveries helped establish General Electric, were two other noted German-Americans of the era. German immigrant John Au-
gustus Roebling designed and built the Brooklyn Bridge, which,
when it was constructed in 1883, ranked as one of the world's
greatest engineering feats. Spanning the East River and connect-
ing Manhattan and Brooklyn, it was the world's first steel-wire
suspension bridge and an engineering marvel of its day.

President Herbert Hoover, whose family surname was originally
spelled Huber, World War I General John Pershing, whose family name had been Persching, and the Rockefellers—who came
to the United States as the Roggenfellers (or Rockenfelders)—
were other Americans of German descent who helped underpin
feelings of German-American pride. Among the other German-
Americans of distinction were George Washington's General
Friedrich Wilhelm von Steuben; Carl Schurz, who fled Germany
after the failed revolution of 1848 and became the first German-
born American elected to the Senate; John Jacob Astor, born Johann Jakob Astor, who became New York's largest real estate
owner and a patron of the arts—the family succeeded in many
businesses—; the piano manufacturer Henry E. Steinway, born

Hermann, Missouri, a town founded by German immigrants in 1842.
Above: The Festhalle, the festival hall, still in operation.
Below: A signpost for Mozart Street, named after the composer.

as Heinrich Engelhard Steinweg; Robert Wagner, who became a senator for New York and helped design the modern welfare state (his son, Robert F. Wagner, was New York City's three-term mayor who ended the reign of Tammany Hall); Walter Chrysler, the founder of Chrysler Motors, whose family came from Germany when an ancestor named Johann Philipp Kreissler immigrated in 1709; newspaper magnates Joseph Pulitzer and Adolph Ochs, theater magnate Oscar Hammerstein I; and the Anheuser-Busch families that created the brewing dynasty. Peter Minuit, who purchased the island of Manhattan on behalf of the Dutch West India Company, was also originally German.

At its peak, the NGAA had 2.5 million members and chapters in all forty-eight states. While it began mainly as an interest group that worked to counter the forces of assimilation and keep German culture alive in America, it later became more political and worked to keep the United States out of the war. But it also became a target of anti-German sentiment, due to its campaign against the Prohibition movement and fund-raising activity for Germany's war relief efforts.

Charles Hexamer, NGAA president from 1901 to 1917, made a fiery speech in Milwaukee on November 22, 1915, which attracted considerable national attention—and also exposed some German-Americans as out of step with the times. "No one will find us prepared to step down to a lesser 'Kultur.' No, we have made it our aim to draw the other up to us," Hexamer said. He also predicted that, although German-Americans were being slandered and persecuted at the time, history would ultimately praise and prize the Germans living in America, "because they will have saved the land from the claws of English tyranny." Hexamer also compared the attacks and discrimination German-Americans faced to the struggles that the earlier American presidents like George Washington and Abraham Lincoln had endured. Hexamer argued that German-Americans had been too modest and too passive in trying to keep the United States out of the war in Europe. "We will not permit our 'Kultur' of 2,000 years to be trodden down . . . we can give our German 'Kultur' to America only if we stand together and conquer the dark spirit of muckerdom and prohibition just as Siegfried once slew the dragon." The NGAA had received a U.S. congressional charter in 1907, but that was revoked in 1918, because of the group's continued campaign to support and defend German culture even in the face of America's wartime hostility toward all things German.

It was not just this kind of German-American arrogance in the air in the United States in the early years of the twentieth century that earned the wrath of other Americans. As historian Richard O'Connor wrote in his 1968 book *The German-Americans: An Informal History*, the NGAA was funded in part by breweries and distilleries and devoted considerable time and effort to the battle against the Anti-Saloon League and that organization's push for a national Prohibition.

The prevailing anti-German sentiment galvanized opponents of alcohol in the United States. The Anti-Saloon League latched on to this unexpected opportunity to help its long-running but so-far unsuccessful crusade to ban alcohol. Purley Baker, president of the Anti-Saloon League, attacked German-Americans as a "race of people who eat like gluttons and drink like swine," and the League was able to raise doubts about the loyalties of German brewers.

There was a distinctly anti-immigrant flavor to the Prohibition movement, which began in the mid-nineteenth century with the rise of the Nativists—it would hurt Italians who were known for their affinity for wine, the Irish and their fondness for whiskey and beer, and the Germans and their taste for beer and liquor. It was a hotly debated issue in the United States for decades, supported by a powerful religious movement against alcohol. Although many areas of the nation were already "dry" by 1914, and antipathy toward Germans was not the only factor in the drive to outlaw alcohol, the movement gained significant momentum and undeniably benefited from the anti-German fever during the war.

William Jennings Bryan published a monthly newspaper called *The Commoner*, a dedicated advocate of Prohibition, which devoted at least half of its articles to the issue. The paper did not conceal its strong views against the National German-American Alliance and its anti-Prohibition stance. Bryant's newspaper tapped into the groundswell of anti-German sentiment in his campaign to outlaw alcohol and root out German influence in the country. One cartoon published in *The Commoner*, entitled "Our 3 Big Enemies," depicted a huge German soldier, a huge Austrian soldier, and a huge bottle of "John Barleycorn" standing menacingly above the Capitol dome. In popular culture, John Barleycorn was a personification of the grain used to make beer and whiskey, as well as the title of Jack London's 1913 book on his own struggle with alcoholism.

But it wasn't until the United States entered World War I that Prohibition finally won enough backing to pass into law. Helped by the anti-German mood, the Senate proposed a nationwide ban on the sale, production, importation, and transport of alcoholic beverages on December 18, 1917—the Eighteenth Amendment. Opposition from powerful German-American ethnic groups helped thwart the Prohibition drive before the war, but in 1917 their influence was on the wane. It took until January 16, 1919, for the necessary thirty-six states to approve the Amendment, which took effect one year later, on January 17, 1920. It was later repealed in 1933, with the ratification of the Twenty-first Amendment.

"The further prolongation of the German-American era was obviously still ardently desired by many Germans in America," Hawgood wrote about the pre-Prohibition efforts to maintain German culture. But, he added, "Time and the passing of the original settlers began to dissolve the hyphen and the breakdown of 'Deutschtum' was beginning to be evident at about the turn of the century: the World War brought to a violent conclusion this process which until then had been a gradual and perhaps scarcely perceptible one."

Historian Richard O'Connor wrote that "German-Americans had every reason to be serenely confident of their place in the national life" in the years prior to World War I. "They had made good; they considered themselves esteemed above all other peoples which had migrated to America from Europe." This prominent role that the Germans were playing in the prewar years led many German-Americans to mistakenly believe that they could prevail against the mainstream in keeping America out of the war in Europe that began in 1914. They were proven wrong.

CHAPTER 3

THE BEGINNING OF THE END: THE VANISHING GERMANS

A focal point of German immigration to the United States was New York City, where many of the newcomers first arrived on ships and ended up staying. The profound German influence in parts of New York served as a microcosm of the role Germans played across the country. In 1900, New York City had the world's second-largest German population, with only Berlin being home to more Germans. More than one-quarter of New York's 3,437,202 residents in 1900 were either of German birth or had one or both parents of German birth. German-language newspapers flourished in the country's biggest and most important city, German clubs were in abundance, the language was taught in many New York schools, and the music of German composers could be heard in concert halls throughout the city. The "Atlantic Garden" in the Bowery was one such popular beer garden that was opened in 1858 by German immigrant Wilhelm Kramer. Before it closed in 1916, crowds of New Yorkers and visitors to the city gathered there to eat German food, drink German beer, listen to German music and party.

Yet by 1963, when Daniel P. Moynihan and Nathan Glazer wrote *Beyond the Melting Pot,* a book about ethnic groups in New York, they noted with some bewilderment that German culture and influence in the city had all but disappeared. "The Germans as a group are vanished. No appeals are made to the German vote, there are no German politicians in the sense that there are Irish or Italian politicians, there are in fact very few Germans in political life, and generally speaking, no German component in the structure of the ethnic interests of the city."

The one million Germans living in New York did not simply disappear. Neither did the eight million Germans living across the country around 1900 just go away. German culture in the United States did, however, all but vanish. The sudden and near complete disappearance of what had been such a vibrant and proud immigrant community in the United States is one of the more phenomenal aspects of twentieth-century immigration and assimilation in the United States. Many immigrants in New York from countries like Italy and Poland retained their native language for several generations into the latter half of the twentieth century, and even third generations of Italian-Americans or Polish-Americans could still speak some Italian or Polish, or at least say a few phrases and prepare ethnic recipes they had picked up from their parents and grandparents. But hardly anyone spoke German after World War I, and even fewer Americans could still speak any German after World War II. The language that was once heard on many street corners at the turn of the century was all but extinct within just a few years.

While *eradication* might seem at first glance like a particularly strong word to describe what happened to German culture in the United States, there is hardly a more apt description. The fate of German culture in America during World War I was due to more than simply the inexorable forces of assimilation. The United States was filling with immigrants from around the world and certainly needed unifying forces, especially during the crisis of wartime. Patriotic fervor helped unite the nation during World War I, but it also unleashed a vengeance against all things German that did much to destroy the previously thriving German-American culture.

The war in Europe broke out on July 28, 1914, triggered by the assassination a month earlier of the heir to the throne of Austria-Hungary, Archduke Franz Ferdinand, and his wife, in the Bosnian capital of Sarajevo. The murderer was Gavrilo Princip, a Serbian student who would become a hero in Serbia. There had been disputes between Austria and the Kingdom of Serbia about control of Bosnia for some time. This led to a diplomatic crisis when Austria-Hungary issued an ultimatum to Serbia and ultimately forced international alliances to be invoked that brought Europe's major powers into what was then known as the Great War.

The Allies, also known as the Triple Entente—Britain, France, and Russia—on the one side, fought against the Central Powers—or Germany and Austria-Hungary—on the other side. Italy, Japan, and the United States later joined the Allies, while the Ottoman Empire (today's Turkey) and Bulgaria later joined the Central Powers. About 65 million soldiers were mobilized for what was one of the world's biggest wars, and more than nine million soldiers were killed by the time it ended on November 11, 1918, as well as seven million civilians.

The war in Europe was an embarrassment for German-Americans. Its first effect was to draw German-Americans closer together, as it served as a temporary check on the further assimilation of German America. "Between 1914 and 1917, German-Americanism, freshly assailed, found new vigor and new cohesion," John Hawgood wrote in *The Tragedy of German-America*. The National German-American Alliance held a rally on August 5 to pass resolutions urging America to stay out of the war.

German-American groups worked tirelessly to keep the United States out of the war in Europe, which was still a fairly popular and mainstream position in 1914 and 1915. But despite that and efforts by President Woodrow Wilson to keep the United States neutral, opinion eventually tipped toward supporting Great Britain, especially as the profitable and economic growth-stimulating export of munitions to Britain and its Allies picked up as the war continued. Trade with Germany, on the other hand, slowed and all but halted because of Britain's highly effective blockade of shipping. Public opinion in the United States increasingly turned against Germany, in part due to Britain's success at spreading propaganda about German military atrocities allegedly committed against civilians in Belgium. At the same time, German-

American newspapers tried to prove that Germany had been an innocent nation forced into war by the revenge-hungry French, an envious Britain, and expansionist Russia, and so the United States became an increasingly polarized nation.

"The outbreak of war in the summer of 1914 came as a thunderclap from a cloudless sky," remarked Carl F. Wittke in his 1936 landmark book, *German-Americans and the World War*. "For the German element it initiated a period of emotional crisis, conflicts of loyalties, misunderstandings, persecutions, and tragedy which few of their fellow citizens appreciated," wrote Wittke, an Ohio historian. Born in 1892 as the son of a German immigrant, Wittke himself endured ethnic discrimination as a young man in his hometown of Columbus, Ohio. Just about everything German in the United States was denounced as part of the "virus of Prussianism." Innocent activities in German clubs, churches, schools, and newspapers were regarded as part of an organized German propaganda effort to try to sweep the United States into the pan-German movement of the Kaiser and his government. Attacks against German-Americans—or "hyphen-hunting" as it was sometimes called—became a popular pastime among extremely patriotic Americans.

The centenary of Otto von Bismarck's birth eight months after the war began, on April 1, 1915, brought leaders of the German-American community together. Many German organizations around the country celebrated the one hundredth anniversary of the birth of the chancellor who united Germany with tributes and expressed their hopes that Bismarck's spirit would help Germany win the war. *The Abendpost* newspaper in Chicago covered a gala and ceremonial toast to the memory of Bismarck, with a remarkably partisan pro-Germany speech, delivered by a speaker named Dr. Lange, and in German.

Otto von Bismarck has forged the Reich together, he has given us internal political unity," a speaker named Dr. Lange said in his opening remarks in German. "Look across the ocean now and behold a people united in their armed strength, waging a war, the kind of which has never been fought before in world history; see them defending themselves against a world of enemies, against a world which knew that it could not stand up to a united Germany in honorable, peaceful competition but instead resorted to war, savagery and murder to weaken and destroy the hateful enemy. He has created a strong and united fatherland for us. United! With courage in our hearts we can face the future confidently. We Germans fear nothing in this world but God. A united Germany is invincible! Dear fatherland! May your righteous cause lead you to victory.

Attitudes like these gave rise to paranoia against German-Americans that cut across all layers of American society. The notion that German spies were swarming the country, of German-American plots, and of various other forms of alleged nefarious subterfuge initiated by German-Americans and Germans living in America became national dialogue. The paranoia also was based on suspected acts of sabotage against American munitions and supply shipments to Britain before the United States joined the war, rather than any real wartime threat, but it nevertheless waxed during the course of the war, unchecked by Congress or the judicial system that instead sometimes even encouraged anti-German sentiment.

On the very day that Robert Paul Prager was lynched in Illinois, for example, a judge in Lafayette County, Kentucky, delivered an angry warning that justice must be meted out against German spies in his state. Kentucky Judge George C. Webb was enraged after learning of the death of horses under mysterious circumstances. The horses were allegedly poisoned, and "German conspirators"—a nebulous foe that could be blamed for many things in that era—were the prime suspects. "Men of this ilk," Webb shouted, "who sow the seeds of dissension or work against the United States government and its people, should be prosecuted, imprisoned, and shot if necessary," according to a report in *The New York Times* on April 5, 1918. "There is not a state in the

Union that is not infested with German spies, and they do not hesitate at anything to spread German propaganda, which is the most villainous, barbarous, and extensive menace that the country has to cope with."

Congressmen also joined in the chorus of criticism against all things German, and one member of the House of Representatives urged a "few prompt hangings" to purge the country of its traitors. "When a seditious or traitorous voice is raised here, I hope the hand of the law will reach out and grasp the speaker," California congressman Julius Kahn said in a speech in a synagogue in Harlem, New York, on March 24, 1918, just twelve days before Prager's death. "I hope that we shall have a few prompt hangings, and the sooner the better. We have got to make an example of a few of these people, and we have got to do it quickly," he said, according to *The New York Times*. The newspaper added that the large audience "cheered wildly" at the point when Kahn called for the hangings.

The final (not as many appear to think, the first) blow to Deutschtum and German-Americanism was the war 1914–17–18," Hawgood concluded. "No longer were the modern Germans able to think of themselves as Americans with a German flavor, or as German-Americans, or as Germans who were born in America. Germans were undesirable aliens, and in 1917 they became enemy aliens; German-Americans were inexplicable and despicable creatures, scorned and spurned by Germany and America alike, while any German flavor was hunted with witch-burning enthusiasm, in which people of German descent were often the most prominent participants. A definite choice had to be made.

One could be either a German or an American, and the former was to be, in 1917, an enemy of the country in which one had been born. The native-born descendants could no longer waver; they were caught between the horns of a dilemma and confronted with an inescapable choice such as had never faced an immigrant stock quite so clearly before.

(. . .) After a final fierce blaze of enthusiasm in the early years of the war, the German-American cause was deserted when America entered the war against Germany.

Historian Frederick Luebke came to a similar conclusion in his 1974 book, *Bonds of Loyalty.* "By 1914 most of the ingredients for an explosive mix were present. The rapidly assimilating German element in America, properly proud of their cultural heritage, had been encouraged by their ethnic chauvinism, by stereotypes native Americans had generally held." With the outbreak of World War I, it became dangerous to be German, and many German-Americans found it prudent to give up or hide their German language and culture. As Hawgood wrote, "The World War, with its hatreds and its persecutions, its propaganda and its coercion, shook the hyphen loose from its moorings and ended the German-American era which had persisted so long. The war brought an abrupt termination to German influence in American life."

"MY COUNTRY, 'TIS OF THEE"
(German-American Version)

My country over sea,
Deutschland, is sweet to me;
    To thee I cling.
For thee my honor died,
For thee I spied and lied,
So that from every side
    Kultur might ring.

Life, 13 June 1918

Left: Another caricature aimed against German-Americans in Life *magazine, accusing them of disloyalty to America.*

Below: A caricature endorsing prohibition directed against German-Americans who were running beer gardens and vineyards.

CHAPTER 4

BOMBS, BULLETS, AND THE RAPE OF BELGIUM

World War I erupted with outbursts of patriotism across Europe in 1914, but it took a while for its effects to be felt in the United States. Violence and discrimination against German-Americans picked up only as the war continued. German-Americans had wielded considerable influence in many areas of the United States at the turn of the century before becoming targets of wrath just a few years later. The origin of the tensions against what had been a respected, accepted, and admired ethnic group is well worth exploring in greater depth. To a certain extent it was a reaction to their determined campaign to keep the United States out of the war. But there were several other reasons why German-Americans went so quickly from being in the mainstream to the margins after World War I began.

A big part of turning American public opinion against Germany—and thus, against German-Americans—was due to British war propaganda. But also Germany did its part to ruin its reputation: German submarines were striking fear into the hearts of Americans by sinking merchant ships crossing the Atlantic, especially the *Lusitania* in 1915. There was also a constant fear in America that German agents and saboteurs were on the loose, and that German-Americans would do their bidding. And whatever lingering affinity Americans might have had for Germany in 1917 was destroyed when it emerged that the German government had secret plans to collaborate with Mexico to invade the United States—as revealed in the Zimmermann telegram.

Fears of German militarism had already been on the rise in the U.S., even more so after a popular book in Europe, titled *Germany and the Next War,* was published. Originally released in Germany in 1911 by General Friedrich von Bernhardi, the book was translated into English and nurtured the unflattering image of Germany as belligerent and all too eager to go to war. Bernhardi spoke out in favor of ruthless aggression and referred to war as a "divine business." His book, which focused on French power as an obstacle to German imperialism, played into the hands of those who worried that there was already a bit too much German culture being preserved in the United States. And especially the reputation of Kaiser Wilhelm II made German-Americans suspicious in the eyes of some Americans. "They suspected that Wilhelm II was prepared to employ any available means, including German-American citizens and organizations, to achieve his objective," Frederick Luebke wrote in *Bonds of Loyalty.*

Those fears multiplied when World War I began with a terrorist act in the Balkans. After the assassination of the archduke in Sarajevo, Austria-Hungary demanded that Serbia hand over Gavrilo Princip. Belgrade refused, and on July 28, 1914, Austria sent troops into Serbia. Russia rushed to help Serbia, whereas Germany sided with its ally Austria. On August 3, Germany and France—Russia's ally—declared war on each other. France had already amassed troops along the German border, and to outflank them, Germany marched into neutral Belgium despite the objections of the Belgian king. Britain protested against the violation of Belgium's neutrality, guaranteed by the 1839 Treaty of London. German Chancellor Theobald von Bethmann Hollweg famously said that he could not believe Britain and Germany would fight a war in 1914 over "a scrap of paper" from 1839. But that's how it happened: The next morning, Britain declared war against Germany. Within only a week, Europe at war.

The United Kingdom did not just mobilize troops—it launched a major propaganda effort that would dwarf everything seen before. Britain's foremost national interest was to get the United States to join its side in the war in Europe—and it did everything to pursue this. The heart of this effort was the War Propaganda Bureau, also known as Wellington House (after its location in London), established in August 1914 under the supervision of the British Foreign Office. The aim was to influence public opinion in neutral countries, especially in the United States. Wellington House enlisted many leading writers in Britain to write books and pamphlets to support the government's positions.

Britain not only controlled the seas with its superior navy, it also had a veritable monopoly on news about the war from Europe to the United States. Not only did the British Navy cut off the delivery of German newspapers, but British agents had also succeeded in locating and cutting the German transatlantic cable to the United States at the bottom of the sea, east of the Azores. This prevented German sources of war news from reaching the United States and created a de-facto monopoly for news from the United Kingdom—an important contributing factor in pushing sentiment in America away from neutrality and against Germany.

Among the British tactics was spreading reports that made Germany's invasion of neutral Belgium appear bestial to neutral countries, with the help of the press as well as the nascent U.S. film industry. The War Propaganda Bureau alone published more than 1,100 pamphlets during World War I, including the controversial "Report on Alleged German Outrages" in 1915, about the allegations of German atrocities in Belgium that helped sway opinion in the United States. British newspapers also began publishing stories portraying the German army as a brutal and barbaric force. The German invasion was called the "Rape of Belgium." British papers wrote that more than one million Belgians were forced to flee and thousands of civilians were killed. Buildings in more than eight hundred towns were damaged or destroyed. Lurid tales of German soldiers bayoneting babies or cutting off the heads, hands, feet, or breasts of women and children, or gouging out the eyes of defenseless civilians were published.

These reports of the barbarism of German soldiers in Belgium had a huge impact on public opinion in the United States, because the stories did not only appear in the UK. They also reverberated

An anti-German World War I poster depicting a German soldier as rapist in Belgium. Those posters spread from the UK to the USA.

in newspaper coverage throughout the United States during the course of the war, particularly in the Midwest, which until then had been so firmly opposed to any American involvement. In an article that appeared in *The Milwaukee Journal* on April 14, 1918, a woman named Florence Clearhout, of Davenport, Iowa, swore in a signed affidavit that while visiting her birthplace in Lendelede, Belgium, in August 1914, she saw German soldiers invade and burn the village, rape women, and cut the hands and fingers off of women and small children for their rings. "I saw a woman carrying two buckets of water," she wrote in her affidavit. "And I saw a soldier pass her and draw his sword and cut off her right hand. I saw a priest plead with the soldiers to spare the lives of women and children, and saw one of the soldiers draw his saber and cut off the priest's head."

The Milwaukee Journal, which had been crusading against German influence in the United States, reported the account from Florence Clearhout as a news item more than four years after it allegedly took place. This and similar, earlier articles helped whip up anti-German sentiment. "I know a young married couple that had retired for the night when five soldiers forced the door of their room and forced the woman to submit to them while the others stood guard over her husband. I know two young girls, eighteen and twenty, who had to submit to the German officers after serving them dinner. I know shortly after this, one of the girls became insane and the other committed suicide." Clearhout also said she saw a French aviator, whose plane had been shot down, dragged from the plane and buried by the Germans while still conscious.

While the stories received attention in the United States, American correspondents arriving in Belgium later struggled to find evidence of atrocities, and there was considerable debate during and after the war about their veracity. Wythe Williams, a *New York Times* correspondent based in Paris, went to the war zone in Belgium to investigate the alleged war crimes and wrote, "None of the rumors of wanton killings and torture could be verified." Williams, who had an accreditation with the French army on the western front, later wrote a book called *Passed by the Censor: The Experience of an American Newspaper Man*. While historians agreed that German soldiers did commit crimes against civilians, sometimes treating them as guerrilla fighters, they generally discounted the reports of atrocities against women and children as exaggerations or outright fabrications. The accounts that reached America at the time, however, left the clear impression that German soldiers were engaging in organized atrocities in Belgium. The famous saying, "The first casualty when war comes is truth," was coined in 1917 by Hiram Johnson, a senator from California who was opposed to U.S. involvement in the war. Johnson's adage is still popular today. World War I reports about German atrocities in Belgium also indirectly contributed to long-term skepticism outside Europe decades later, when reports of mass murders at Nazi concentration camps first emerged. At first, many feared that they were being duped again.

Britain's Wellington House also turned to the nascent film industry to try to influence the debate in neutral countries, especially the United States. In 1915, it recruited Charles Urban, an American filmmaker of German ancestry, to produce a documentary film called *Britain Prepared*. Urban, who was born in Cincinnati in 1867 as Carl Urban, was also involved in making the 1916 documentary *The Battle of the Somme*, a propaganda film he edited, which depicted in heroic style what it was like to be in trench warfare. Urban also edited the British government's newsreel, *Official War Review*. The same year, Britain set up the War Office Cinematograph Committee that later became part of the Department of Information, based in London. It released films aimed specifically at pushing the United States into the war, such as *The Tanks in Action at the Battle of the Ancre*, and *The Retreat of the Germans at the Battle of Arras*.

In a similar vein, albeit somewhat later, the American film industry produced a number of propaganda films to try to rally support behind the war effort. This happened mostly after the United States declared war on Germany in 1917. *The Kaiser, the Beast of Berlin* was a 1918 silent feature film that portrayed Kaiser Wilhelm as an unsavory tyrant who faced resistance from his own soldiers. *America Goes Over* was a documentary propaganda film produced by the U.S. Army in 1918, depicting American troops in Europe under the command of General John J. Pershing. *The*

Bond was another propaganda film by Charlie Chaplin, designed to drum up support for Liberty Bonds, war bonds sold in the United States to support the war effort of the Allies. It was a series of humorous sketches strung together, and in the final scene, the character played by Chaplin uses a giant hammer with the words "Liberty Bonds" written on it to symbolically "knock out" the Kaiser. While Chaplin is remembered today as a Hollywood actor, he was a British citizen. Another film, *Battling Jane*, was a silent melodrama about a woman who raises funds to buy Liberty Bonds and to donate to the Red Cross.

All those efforts turned public opinion in many parts of the United States, especially on the East Coast, against Imperial Germany. This growing antagonism was gaining even more momentum when Germany started submarine attacks on British ships in the Atlantic. Britain and Germany both relied heavily on imported food supplies and munitions—largely from the United States and North America. But Germany, blockaded by the superior British Navy, struggled to get much-needed supplies and food from its trading partners and struggled to cope with Britain's "hunger blockade," as it is known in Germany. American and British historians have estimated that at least 425,000 German civilians starved to death, because of the blockade, many of them children. German authorities put the death toll attributed to the tight trade sanctions at more than 760,000.

In an attempt to fight back against Britain's control of the Atlantic, the German military began to turn increasingly to its deadly new weapon: the submarine. The "U-Boote" were silent, undetectable, and deadly. German submarines sank a number of British ships—merchant as well as military—in the opening months of the war. All in all, some five thousand ships were torpedoed by German submarines in the Atlantic and Mediterranean. But in the early years of the war, Germany put self-imposed limits on the use of its submarines because it did not want to provoke the United States into getting involved on the side of the Allies.

The tensions in the Atlantic worsened in 1915. A German submarine sank a small, unarmed British ship called the *Falaba* on

March 2, and one American on board died—the first American civilian casualty of the war. A month later, an American oil tanker, the *Gulflight*, was torpedoed and three Americans were killed in the explosion on board. As the debate in America grew on whether or not the sinking of ships, armed or otherwise, was a violation of international law, the *Lusitania* was torpedoed by a German submarine on May 7, 1915, and quickly sank. The British ocean liner was sailing through the war zone under an American flag and went down off the coast of Ireland. Of the 1,198 people killed, 128 were Americans.

Germany tried to defend the attack by pointing out that the ship had sunk so quickly, in just eighteen minutes, even before many of its lifeboats could be released, because it was loaded with heavy munitions. In fact, the *Lusitania* had—as *The New York Times* revealed the day after the sinking— about 4,200,000 rounds of rifle cartridges, 1,250 empty shell cases, and eighteen cases of fuses on board. In addition, the ship had been declared an armed merchant cruiser. The German Embassy had even placed ads beforehand in about fifty American newspapers, including *The New York Times*, in April 1915, warning travelers on British ships that they were passing through a war zone and doing so at their own peril. The warning ran next to a Cunard lines ad soliciting passengers for the *Lusitania's* doomed voyage.

Notice!

Travellers intending to embark on the Atlantic voyage are reminded that a state of war exists between Germany and her allies and Great Britain and her allies; that the zone of war includes the waters adjacent to the British Isles; that, in accordance with formal notice given by the Imperial German Government, vessels flying the flag of Great Britain, or any of her allies, are liable to destruction in those waters and that travellers sailing in the war zone on the ships of Great Britain or her allies do so at their own risk.

Imperial German Embassy,
Washington, D.C., April 22, 1915.

Literary Digest, **22 May 1915**

The German Embassy warned passengers of the Lusitania and other ships traveling to England in an ad placed in The New York Times.

The advance warnings did nothing to placate or neutralize America's anger over the ship's sinking. On the contrary, the advertisement made it seem to some as if the submarine attack had been premeditated. "No event in World War I stirred American emotions more profoundly," Luebke wrote. "Appalled by the destruction of civilian life, most Americans condemned the sinking as a revolting crime against humanity." Luebke believes the sinking also had a chilling effect on German nationals living in the United States, leading to a fourfold increase in German aliens applying

55

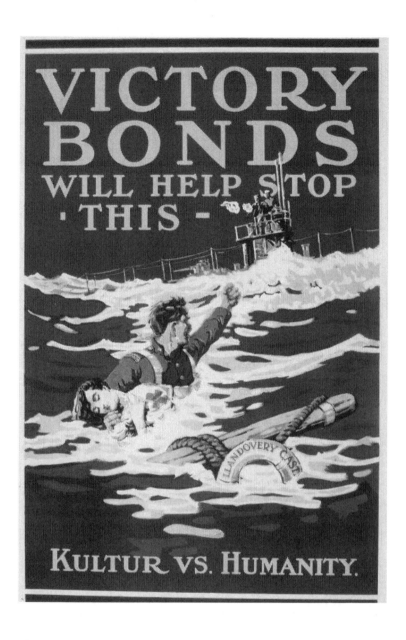

Even after the United States entered World War I, the 1915 sinking of the Lusitania *was frequently used as a symbol of German inhumanity in posters, pictures, postcards, newspaper photos, and stamps.*

for U.S. citizenship that year. The sinking of the *Lusitania* further exacerbated hostility toward German-Americans and drew the United States ever closer to joining the war against Germany.

Luebke observed that the majority of German-language newspapers deplored the sinking, although many continued to argue that the United States should remain neutral despite the attack. Reflecting the intense pro-German passions in some parts of German-influenced America, a few German-language newspapers even celebrated the ship's sinking. The *Cincinnati Volksblatt* wrote that the "torpedoing of the *Lusitania* was a shot straight into the heart of England." The *Volksblatt* added that the nearly 1,200 killed on the *Lusitania* paled in comparison to the estimated 100,000 German soldiers who would have been slaughtered if the munitions carried by the ship had reached the battlefield.

Though many Americans were still wary about joining Europe's war, the country was losing patience with Imperial Germany over the sinking of merchant ships. There was no shortage of articles in American periodicals following the 1915 *Lusitania* incident that portrayed German-Americans as a threat to national security, an enemy within. But even though the sinking of the *Lusitania* pushed the United States toward war, it would take another two years before the country declared war on Germany.

President Woodrow Wilson, a Democrat, faced a difficult re-election campaign in 1916. The embattled president was generally not expected to win a second term. His campaign was centered on the premise that "He kept us out of the war." Wilson faced a delicate balancing act: keeping the United States neutral despite the growing ill will toward Germany after the *Lusitania* sinking. Many German-Americans had renounced loyalty to Germany and pledged their allegiance to the United States. The *St. Paul Volkszeitung* published an editorial that reflected the shifting mood in the German-speaking community. "No matter how great the suffering and mental agony that German-Americans would undergo, there can be no question about their loyalty to the stars and stripes."

The leader of a group called the "German Veterans Alliance of North America" said that, if necessary, German-Americans would not hesitate to take up arms against Germany. The "German Catholic Union of Baltimore" voted to express its undivided loyalty to the United States, and scores of other German-American societies adopted similar measures. The pledges of fealty by German-Americans were nevertheless too little, too late, and the fervor to eradicate everything German from the United States was only gaining momentum. Another source of tension stirring fears about the loyalty of German-Americans were acts of sabotage against munitions plants, depots, and British-bound ships carrying munitions and food supplies during America's neutrality period before 1917. Attacks on American munitions plants and depots by German agents and German sympathizers were designed mainly to thwart the flow of weapons to Britain and its Allies, and to keep the United States distracted, occupied, and out of the war.

American arms makers had no compunctions about selling their weapons and munitions to belligerents on both sides of the war, and the U.S. government had no desire to limit weapons trade, as the war in Europe had stimulated urgently needed U.S. economic growth. The United States did not want to let a simple detail like neutrality get in the way of its business interests. But by 1915, Britain's naval blockade effectively shut down trade between American firms and Germany and its allied Central Powers. American arms makers ended up selling almost all of the munitions they produced to Britain, France, and Russia, and their factories were kept busy filling orders from just the one side.

As long as the United States stayed neutral, there was little fallout after incidents of sabotage. Wilson was trying to keep the United States out of the war and had no interest in leading a public campaign against German agents on the loose and operating surreptitiously in the United States. Germans were nevertheless responsible for a number of high-profile sabotage acts. The earlier attacks by a fairly small number of saboteurs later gave Americans reason to doubt the loyalty of the entire ethnic German community.

The attacks were often directed against munitions, bridges, chemical plants, and military matériel produced in the U. S. slated to be shipped to the Allies in Europe. The acts of sabotage were sometimes executed in clumsy fashion by amateurs, investigations later revealed. Easy recruits were idled German sailors stranded in New York Harbor because their merchant vessels were unable to leave the United States for fear of being attacked by the British Navy. Four men working at a munitions factory in Jersey City, New Jersey, were killed in an explosion at the Detwiller Street munitions factory, and in Pompton Lakes a Dupont powder mill was attacked.

German agents started fires on supply ships, sowed unrest in ordnance factories, and damaged shipping infrastructure wherever possible. One device used frequently for attacks was known as the "cigar bomb." These small and rather crude devices had time-delay fuses and were placed strategically on cargo ships to start fires in the hulls and disable or destroy the ships as they crossed the Atlantic. They were called cigar bombs because they were shaped like a cigar and contained acid on one side and explosive material on the other, with a thin copper plate separating the two ends. It took about a week for the acid to erode through the copper plate and ignite a fire—usually when the ships were in middle of the Atlantic. Irish stevedores in New York Harbor, who often had little sympathy for the British, were recruited by German agents to secretly plant the cigar bombs among flammable cargo items, such as sacks of sugar, on Britain-bound ships. It was all but impossible to determine the cause of the fire after the ships burned and usually sank somewhere in the middle of the ocean.

Another chilling case of sabotage that increased Americans' fear of attack at home involved a German-American named Anton Dilger, a physician whose father, Hubert Dilger, had earned a Medal of Honor during the Civil War. Anton Dilger went to Germany to study and later became a surgeon in the German Army. He was upset by the fact that Wilson claimed the United States was neutral while it sold munitions to Britain and France. Because he was an American citizen, Dilger offered to return to the United States in 1915 and work as a "germ saboteur."

He set up a laboratory in Chevy Chase, Maryland, where he produced anthrax and other bacteria intended to kill horses and livestock in transit from the United States to Europe, according to Robert Koenig in *The Fourth Horseman*, 2007. In addition to the flow of munitions to Britain and France, the U.S. was also selling thousands of horses to the Allies, who used them to cart supplies and artillery weapons. Stevedores in several U.S. ports were paid by German agents to inoculate horses bound for Europe by applying the bacteria to their nostrils. But Dilger's germ-warfare plan was a failure, most likely due to incorrect application of the bacteria.

Other incidents further raised fears of the threat of German-Americans and eroded Americans' confidence in their German neighbors, including a series of bizarre crimes committed in July 1915 by Eric Muenter. There has been speculation that Muenter, a German nationalist who had previously taught German at Harvard University, might have been a German agent with financial backing from the German government, but that was never incontrovertibly proven. Muenter's back-to-back acts of terror on consecutive days in 1915 showed, in any case, how unprotected Americans and their institutions were a century ago. Muenter, who was also known by various aliases, including Erich Muenter and Frank Holt, was also upset that the United States was supplying weapons to just the Allied side, making a farce of its neutrality pledge, and he was angry that American bankers, like J. P. Morgan, were helping Britain finance its war effort against his native Germany.

Muenter first traveled to Washington, where he intended to place a small bomb in the vacant Senate Chamber during the Fourth of July holiday. But he found the doors to the chamber locked, so he left his package, containing three sticks of dynamite, under the telephone switchboard operator's unoccupied desk in the adjacent Senate Reception Chamber. He set the timer of his bomb to explode just before midnight on July 2, 1915. Muenter then walked to the rail station to catch the overnight train to New York. He heard the explosion at the Capitol Building while waiting on the rail platform. The detonation was not large but still managed to break mirrors, windows, chandeliers, and damage the ceiling, according to William C. Allen's *History of the United States Capitol: A Chronicle of Design, Construction and Politics*, 2001. Muenter had sent a letter to the editor of the *Washington Evening Star*, using an as-

Another Life *magazine caricature called for German-American
saboteurs to be put before firing squads.*

sumed name, in which he claimed responsibility for the attack. In the letter, which was published after the attack, Muenter wrote of his hope that the explosion "would make enough noise to be heard above the voices that clamor for war [and be] an exclamation point in [his] appeal for peace."

But Muenter was not yet finished. Upon arriving in New York by train the following morning, he went to the poorly guarded Long Island estate of John Pierpoint Morgan Jr., whose bank was playing a major role in financing the Allies. Son of the legendary financier and philanthropist J. P. Morgan, he had lent $12 million to Russia in 1914, and $50 million to France in 1915. His close involvement with British and French wartime interests led to suspicion in the United States that his bank was trying to push the United States into the war so he could get his money back. He later organized a syndicate of more than two thousand banks that lent a total of $500 million to the Allies. J. P. Morgan Jr.'s company also acted as the British government's purchasing agent in the United States and ordered everything, from steel to food, for Britain's war effort.

Muenter went to Morgan's house in Glen Cove, New York, intending to protest Morgan's profiteering from the war and to push for an embargo on arms exports to Britain. When Morgan opened the door, Muenter pulled out his pistol and shot Morgan twice in the groin. The wounds were superficial, though, and Morgan soon recovered. Muenter, however, was captured and arrested. He committed suicide in prison a few days later, under mysterious circumstances. Muenter's attempted assassination of J. P. Morgan Jr. convinced many Americans that Germans living in America could resort to any means, including anarchy.

Some newspapers argued that all German- and Austrian-born Americans should be treated as spies unless their innocence could be otherwise proven—an unusual view of justice and due process. There were reports of German submarines secretly placing spies on the East Coast, and fears that German agents were contaminating food, poisoning the water, sabotaging munitions factories, and even spreading germs. The Justice Department investigated hundreds of reports, but not a single German spy was even arrested, let alone tried or convicted during the war years. But tensions remained high. The Austrian ambassador, Konstantin Dumba, was declared persona non grata and forced to leave Washington two months after the Dilger incidents, when, in September 1915, his involvement in sabotage schemes against munitions factories and fomenting strikes was uncovered. Dumba had bluntly warned all Austro-Hungarian citizens living in the United States that they would be considered guilty of treason if they worked in factories supplying enemy countries with weapons or munitions. While some German-language newspapers protested his removal, arguing that the United States was hardly neutral by supplying only Britain and its Allies but not Germany, many others, including the *New York Herald* and the *Illinois Staats-Zeitung*, supported the president for expelling the Austrian ambassador.

Diplomatic blunders by Germans further exacerbated tensions prior to U.S. involvement in the war. Franz von Papen was a German military attaché in Washington caught red-handed in 1915, trying to recruit idled German seamen, stranded in New York when their ships were interned, to moonlight as saboteurs and spies. Von Papen encouraged them to participate in clandestine missions to blow up bridges, piers, canals, and other strategic infrastructure targets. Von Papen's undercover work made a farce of his diplomatic status, and he was expelled from the United States. In 1916, a year after his ejection, von Papen was indicted in absentia for his involvement in a plot to blow up the Welland Canal that circumvents Niagara Falls and connects Lake Ontario and Lake Erie. The plot, however, had failed. His bungled diplomatic service did not hurt von Papen's German career. Back in Germany, he later became chancellor for a short while, in 1932, before becoming vice-chancellor under Adolf Hitler in 1933.

It was also later revealed that also Germany's well-known ambassador, a veritable celebrity in the United States at the time, named Count Johann Heinrich von Bernstorff, had been secretly involved in the planning of some of the attacks—despite his public efforts to maintain peace and keep the United States out of the war. Von Bernstorff had been summoned to Germany on July 14,

1914, when he was recruited to conduct intelligence operations in the United States, according to Howard Blum's book *Dark Invasion 1915: Germany's Secret War and the Hunt for the First Terrorist Cell in America*, 2014. The ambassador was given $150 million to finance the network of agents and sabotage activities. He returned to the United States on August 2 with his huge slush fund.

Bernstorff was involved in a number of bombing plots before he was ordered to leave in February 1917, when the United States severed its diplomatic ties to Germany. Among them was the attempted sabotage of the Welland Canal in Upstate New York, the explosion of the Roebling Wire and Cable plant in New Jersey in 1915, and the bombing of an American merchant ship carrying wheat in 1915. The most notorious act of terrorism, however, in which the ambassador was at least indirectly involved, was the explosion at Black Tom Island in 1916. Black Tom, an island located between New York and New Jersey, was America's most important munitions depot in World War I, where railcars unloaded about three-quarters of the ammunition produced in the United States onto ships bound for Europe.

On July 30, 1916, German agents managed to sneak into the poorly guarded depot that contained two million pounds of explosives and set a series of fires. The fires were discovered by the night watchmen. But the watchmen quickly fled the danger zone. Two hours later, at 2 a.m. the depot erupted in a massive explosion. It was so powerful that it shook the earth, measuring 5.5 on the Richter scale. The blast was heard and felt as far south as Maryland and as far north as Connecticut. It shattered windows across the Hudson River in Manhattan and dozens of miles away, described by Jules Witcover in his book, *Sabotage at Black Tom: Imperial Germany's Secret War in America, 1914–1917*.

Suddenly a thunderous blast shattered the calm and the night turned into day," "After the first jolt, an eerie quiet settled for a moment on New York Harbor and the city … Then, panic-stricken residents of Manhattan's teeming tenements, and those in Jersey City, Bayonne and Hoboken on the New Jersey side, threw open their windows and craned for a view of the orange-red heavens. As they gawked, the bombardment resumed as if the harbor itself were under attack from some mighty, invisible armada. It continued undiminished for about twenty minutes, when a second stupendous explosion rocked the buildings on both sides of the river, unleashing yet another tremendous fusillade into the sky. All at once, greater New York was alive, as thousands upon thousands of people poured into the streets, bewildered. Flaming rockets and screeching shells pierced the sky, like a great fireworks display, illuminating Miss Liberty from torch to base. Beyond her, the tip of Manhattan and much of the world's most spectacular skyline instantly were awash in light. With the huge explosion, the whole harbor seemed to shudder, sending shock waves pounding against skyscraper windows, shattering them by the thousands and sending deadly splinters of glass plunging into the streets and sidewalks below. Shrapnel pellets tore into the giant statue and ripped gaping holes in the walls of the buildings on nearby Ellis Island, terrifying newly arrived immigrants who thought they had escaped the Great War in Europe.

At least seven people were killed and hundreds more injured in the worst terrorist attack to that point in the United States. Damage to the Statue of Liberty and other property in the region was estimated at $20 million—or the equivalent of some $400 million in 2014. "Late-night revelers in Brooklyn were knocked down and sleepers were thrown from their beds," Witcover wrote. "A ten-week-old boy, Arthur Tosson, was hurled from his crib in Jersey City to his death. And incredibly, as far south as Philadelphia, others were awakened by what they feared was an earthquake—or worse. Police in towns even farther south, in Maryland, received inquiries about the mysterious disturbance."

At first it was assumed that the explosion at Black Tom had been an accident, and President Wilson's administration had little interest in any explanation other than accidental fire. Several investigations into who was responsible for the gigantic explo-

The Zimmermann telegram was intercepted by British intelligence.

sion followed, one of the first for the embryonic Federal Bureau of Investigation (in 1916, the FBI was still a small, young organization, with just 260 employees). For a while, an Irish group opposed to Britain was thought to be involved. It took a while before suspicion turned to Germany—it wasn't until 1939 that a German-American Mixed Claims Commission ruled that Imperial Germany was responsible for the attack and ordered that damages be paid to the Leigh Valley Railroad Company that was devastated during the incident. In 1953, the two sides reached a settlement, with West Germany agreeing to pay $50 million in damages.

TELEGRAM RECEIVED.

FROM 2nd from London # 5747.

"We intend to begin on the first of February
unrestricted submarine warfare. We shall endeavor
in spite of this to keep the United States of
America neutral. In the event of this not succeed-
ing, we make Mexico a proposal of alliance on the
following basis: make war together, make peace
together, generous financial support and an under-
standing on our part that Mexico is to reconquer
the lost territory in Texas, New Mexico, and
Arizona. The settlement in detail is left to you.
You will inform the President of the above most
secretly as soon as the outbreak of war with the
United States of America is certain and add the
suggestion that he should, on his own initiative,
invite Japan to immediate adherence and at the same
time mediate between Japan and ourselves. Please
call the President's attention to the fact that
the ruthless employment of our submarines now
offers the prospect of compelling England in a
few months to make peace." Signed, ZIMMERMANN.

The British turned over the decoded, translated text to the United States.

The final—but without a doubt the most important—factor that
unleashed a tidal wave of anti-German sentiment and brought
the United States into the Great War in Europe was what became
known as the Zimmermann telegram. As terrifying as submarine
warfare had been, nothing came even close to upsetting Americans as much as the telegram from Arthur Zimmermann, Germany's deputy foreign minister in Berlin.

With the German Army stuck in a trench warfare stalemate, and
after years of debate among German leaders on whether the military should let its submarines go all out to try to win the war, at

the risk of drawing the United States in, the pro-submarine faction prevailed. It argued that the war could be won within months if the submarines had a free hand against Britain, before the United States had a chance to play any decisive role. In a secret telegram dated January 13, 1917, Zimmermann sent a coded message from Berlin to Germany's ambassador in Washington, to be forwarded to the German ambassador in Mexico, warning that Germany would renew its unrestricted submarine warfare against all ships passing through the war zone in the Atlantic, effective February 1. That would quite likely draw the United States into the war.

What made the Zimmermann telegram especially disturbing to Americans, however, was another part of the message. Zimmermann instructed the ambassador in Mexico City to "propose an alliance with Mexico," and to persuade Mexico to invade the United States. That would tie up the United States militarily on its southern border and divert attention away from the war in Europe. Germany could offer Mexico "generous financial support" and would allow Mexico to recover the "lost territories of New Mexico, Texas and Arizona."

Though half a century had passed since the Mexican-American War of 1846–1848, triggered by U.S. annexation of Texas in 1845, tensions were still running high between Mexico and the United States. During that war, American soldiers also took control of New Mexico, Arizona, parts of Utah and Colorado, and most of California. Relations between the United States and Mexico were especially tense in 1916, after Mexico's revolutionary general Pancho Villa raided the U.S. border town of Columbus, New Mexico. Villa's forces burned and looted many of the houses before they were quickly driven back south of the border in a full-scale battle with the U.S. Army. The Mexican raid angered the United States, and Wilson sent an expeditionary force, led by General John J. Pershing, into Mexico to try to capture Villa. Pershing was only called back to the United States in 1917, when the United States declared war on Germany.

The German government hoped to capitalize on Mexico's soured relations with the United States and hoped that an alliance with Mexico would tie up American resources and keep the United States pinned down in its own backyard on its southern border. But British intelligence intercepted the Zimmermann telegram, deciphered it, and turned it over to President Wilson. On March 1, the Wilson administration released the Zimmermann telegram to the Associated Press news agency, and newspapers across the country published stories on it.

The telegram's contents shocked the United States, including German-Americans. Many German-language newspaper editors initially expressed doubt about the accuracy of the reports and found it unfathomable that the German minister could possibly even consider assisting a Mexican invasion of the United States. German-language newspapers denounced it as a forgery, as just another effort by the same British propaganda agents who had spread the atrocity stories about Belgium earlier in the war, and a fabrication to force the United States into the war. But on March 29, when Zimmermann himself confirmed the contents of the intercepted telegram, German newspaper editors were stunned. Many immediately abandoned their support for Germany.

"If what is beyond all belief should prove to be true, no American, whatever his descent or nationality, will hesitate for a moment in performing his full duty to his country," wrote the *Cincinnati Volksblatt*. Most German-language newspapers that had argued for years against American participation in the war did an about-face after the Zimmermann telegram. Their reversal, however, was too little, too late for many Americans, who were already deeply suspicious of their German-American compatriots. The specter of Mexican forces invading Texas, New Mexico, and Arizona, with the support and encouragement of Imperial Germany, pushed the United States into the war.

Wilson asked Congress for a declaration of war against Germany four days later, on April 2, 1917. The Senate voted 82–6 for war, on April 4, and the House of Representatives approved the measure by a 373–50 margin on April 6. Wilson signed the declaration later that day. It was only the third time in U.S. history that a president had asked Congress for a declaration of war.

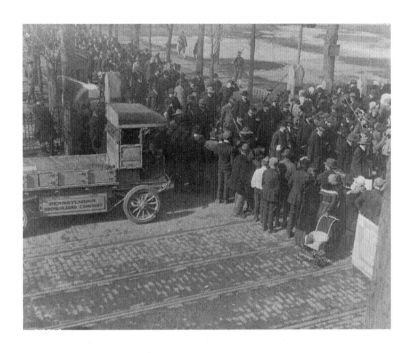

Above: German-Americans taken to an internment camp in Pennsylvania.
Below: Barracks at the internment camp in Fort Douglas, Utah.

On the same day that Wilson asked Congress for a declaration of war, Alexander Bannwart, a pacifist of Swiss-German ancestry and former minor-league baseball player in Boston, reportedly punched pro-war senator Henry Cabot Lodge during a widely reported encounter outside the senator's office. Bannwart summoned Lodge from his office with a group of pacifists and urged him to vote against the war declaration. At some point during their conversation, Bannwart reportedly called Lodge a coward, and Lodge called Bannwart a liar. It was initially reported that Bannwart then hit Lodge, and the sixty-seven-year-old senator responded by punching the thirty-six-year-old Bannwart in the jaw. The scuffle was quickly broken up, but reports of their fight made the front page nationwide, and the elderly Lodge was feted for taking on his younger nemesis. Bannwart later charged Lodge for assault and $20,000 in damages, *The New York Times* reported on May 10; as part of his settlement of the suit two years later, Lodge admitted that he had struck Bannwart first.

Pent-up enthusiasm for the war led to a surge of patriotism when the war declaration finally came. In a speech on Flag Day, June 14, 1917, which was meant to justify American entry into the war—against the German military, but not the German people—President Wilson's unusually belligerent language did its part to ignite this fervor. "The military masters of Germany have filled our unsuspecting communities with vicious spies and conspirators and have sought to corrupt the opinion of our people," Wilson said. "They seek to undermine the government with false professions of loyalty to its principles."

Shortly after declaring war on Imperial Germany in April 1917, Wilson placed new restrictions on male, German-born American residents aged fourteen and older. About 250,000 German-born men were required to register their address and employment at a local post office. A year later in April 1918 the Wilson Administration's requirement was extended to include all German-born women as well. About 6,000 of those were arrested, and 2,000 were sent to internment camps—one in Fort

Oglethorpe, Georgia, and another in Fort Douglas, Utah, near Salt Lake City.

The 2,000 "dangerous Germans" were held for the duration of the war under the Department of Justice's Enemy Alien Registration Section, an agency managed by a young J. Edgar Hoover long before he became the director of the FBI. They were subjected to interrogation and investigations. Some Germans traveling in the United States also got swept into the camps. A German geneticist, Richard Goldschmidt, was on a study trip to Japan 1914 but he got stranded in the United States on his way to Germany and was eventually interned in a camp until 1918. He returned to Germany in 1919 but then, as a Jew, fled Germany in 1935 to the United States. He became a well-known professor at the University of California.

The camps for Germans and treatment during detention were not in the same notorious league as the much larger internment camps set up during World War II, where some 120,000 Japanese and Japanese-Americans were held. The Germans interned in the United States were not forced to sell their property and were in general treated with more dignity, although they had to submit to forced labor. Most were released in June 1919 on parole thanks to a decree from Attorney General A. Mitchell Palmer, although some were detained until April 1920.

There was another group of Germans detained during World War I—crew members of German commercial vessels. There were about 2,200 merchant sailors on 54 German vessels stranded at ports in the United States in early 1917 due to the British blockade. They were detained as prisoners of war. Most were interned on the grounds of the Mountain Park Hotel in Hot Springs, North Carolina—a town with a population of just 650. The hotel's owner had won a lucrative deal from the War Department to house the German sailors. Officers and crew of what was then the world's biggest ship, the *Vaterland*, were held in Hot Springs.

In highly charged atmosphere following the declaration of war, even fires of uncertain origin were suddenly blamed on "German-American plots." One 1918 blaze that destroyed about three city blocks in Kansas City was originally suspected of hav-

Above: German-American mayors and other luminaries as they entered an internment camp in Georgia. Below: The camp's sleeping hall.

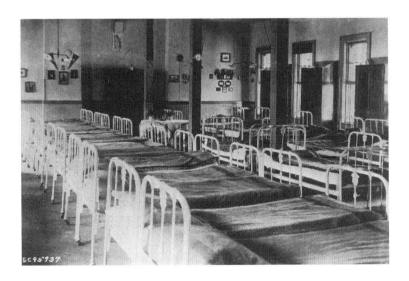

Above: A picture of the "Literarischer Zirkel" (Literary Circle) at the Fort Douglas internment camp that attempted to show prisoners were being well treated. Below: This is what prisoners actually did —forced labor.

ing been started by an arsonist. In the weeks following the blaze, there were numerous reports in national newspapers that "enemy agents" were responsible. The source of information that fueled the speculation that German agents could be on the loose in Kansas City was James Marvin, the city's fire warden. "I grew suspicious when it was called to my attention that the fire had burned against the wind," Marvin was quoted by *The New York Times* on April 6, 1918. "Almost as soon as the fire was discovered, other fires began to break out in adjacent buildings. That would indicate that they were deliberately started." Marvin went further by saying that because there were warehouses of food supplies nearby—even though the fire never got close to those warehouses—that was "proof" that there was a plot by enemy agents to set the other buildings on fire.

It is not difficult to find similar stories in American newspapers in the spring of 1918, of fires being blamed on nefarious German spies. But what is difficult to find are stories that determined the actual causes of many of these the fires and whether fire damage nationwide really did rise sharply. *The Nation* magazine reported in March 1918 that fire damage was indeed on the rise after the United States declared war on Germany, but it noted that investigators often attributed the blazes to the increased pressures of wartime production rather than saboteurs. *The Nation* noted that popular hysteria found it convenient to blame "German agents" for increased fire losses but pointed out that a report from the Board of Fire Underwriters, an agency that worked to prevent fires at the turn of the century, wrote in its March 28, 1918, issue that only six out of seventy-five of the nation's largest fires in the previous year had been of genuinely "suspicious origin." The Board of Fire Underwriters acknowledged that it could not find any evidence that German saboteurs were responsible for the increase in fire damage.

"Even the waterfront fire at Baltimore last October [1917], so confidently alleged to have been set by a German spy, was proven of other origin," *The Nation* noted. The article referred to the Board's report, which cited the primary reason for escalating fire losses as being the "hastily enlarged facilities, night and day shift, employment of inexperienced labor, crowded storage spaces, and high general pressure circumstances."

Fear and paranoia about Germans was clearly on the rise in Spring 1918. New York City newspapers began reporting on stories about tiny bits of glass found in loaves of bread and bottles of milk. The articles pointed fingers at German saboteurs, even though federal investigators ruled that out a few weeks later. But the damage had been done. Fear that German agents were resorting to sabotaging America's food supply gripped the nation. *The New York Times* quoted several eyewitnesses who pinned the blame for the glass particles on "German agents" in articles that are chilling to read even a century later.

Yet after investigating twelve reports of glass fragments in food in the New York area, United States Marshall James M. Power determined that there was no evidence to prove a widespread plot and added that the "pieces of glass" turned out to be sand or other substances. Power said there was only one case investigated in which glass bits were found embedded in bread crust, and German agents were first suspected. But it turned out that a window in the bakery had accidentally been broken a week earlier, and the glass particles had come from that incident. Glass particles found in milk bottles turned out to be from rough handling of the bottles, which resulted in chipped rims, and were not the work of enemy aliens. Power said that "glass" found in candy had proven to be crystallized sugar.

The story on the real causes of the glass in the food supply was buried deep inside *The New York Times* in a short, four-paragraph item at the bottom of page fifteen, under the headline, "More hysteria than glass: "US Marshall finds no German plot to make food dangerous to life"—in contrast to the front-page coverage of earlier reports of enemy plots responsible for glass chips found in food. That everything from "mysterious fires" to glass chips found in milk bottles could be blamed on German-Americans shows how extensive the hysteria had become.

CHAPTER 5

500,000 LAMPPOSTS TO HANG GERMAN-AMERICANS

The situation deteriorated rapidly for German-Americans after the U.S. declaration of war. Many German-Americans had campaigned long and hard against U.S. involvement but were suddenly on the wrong side of history and became easy prey for patriotic Americans.

The general fear of German spies and saboteurs running rampant in the United States only worsened after the country entered the war. "We are at war. The German people, whom we have been implored not to hate, with devilish cunning are daily committing murder and arson, impeding military preparation by crippling factories and machinery, killing men and women without compunction," read a February 1918 article in the *North American Review,* called "Kill Spies." "The time for sentiment has passed, the time for action has come," the article continued, further arguing that spies knew what the penalty for espionage was: death. And the United States should thus not continue to allow spies to be tried in civilian courts, "where justice is uncertain and legal technicalities govern," but rather should try spies before a court-martial. "A single spy shot will deter a score," the *North American Review* concluded.

Although many of the wartime sabotage allegations were later determined to be false, there was no shortage of articles in newspapers and magazines urging Americans to be on the watch and do their own part to uncover German activities. "What is needed in this country now is militant patriotism," Cleveland Moffett wrote in the November 1917 issue of *McClure's*, a monthly illustrated magazine that was popular at the time. "We cannot face the immediate menace of treason and sedition with the calm detachment of a professor of Constitutional Law who would let his house burn down while he searched the records to decide whether it was justifiable, in the absence of a fire department, to organize a bucket brigade."

In one especially vitriolic article in the July 1917 issue of *Mc-Clure's*, U.S. Army Sergeant Arthur Guy Empey urged Americans to go all-out against Germans in Europe and at home. "We are not fighting Prussianism and Militarism alone. We are at war with Germany, the German people, and everything connected with Germany." Empey said that Americans did not need to fear the German-American who "goes out into the street and shouts 'Hoch der Kaiser'" ("Hooray for the Kaiser") for this type of traitor will land in a hospital, and when he wakes we can put him to sleep again." Empey said that the truly dangerous German-Americans, the ones that "we have to watch and exterminate," were the German-Americans who wore American flags on their breast pockets but secretly harbored loyalty for the Kaiser. He told readers that, empowered by the Espionage and Sedition Act, every American had the authority to arrest anyone who utters pro-German or anti-Ally statements. "Constitute yourself a secret-service agent, and if at any time you hear a remark against our government or against our allies, no matter how trivial or unimportant it may seem to you, either arrest that person or report his or her name and address."

Describing German-Americans as a "parasite on the folds of the star-spangled banner," Empey tore into the continued use of the German language on American streets. "If a man cannot speak English, and can only speak German, that man must be an enemy of the United States because he does not understand this wonderful democracy of ours. But if a man can speak English and prefers to speak German, then since it is war time, that man must be doubly an enemy of the United States."

Empey further advised readers to "butt right into the middle of any such conversations in German that they heard going on around them. There was no satisfactory reason for people speaking German in the United States," Empey insisted, adding, "I cannot tell you what I would do, but if you are a true American, you will know. There is a slogan in this war that says, 'If you can't fight over there, fight over here.'"

Empey found it simply revolting that American soldiers returning home from the war in Europe could still see German-language newspapers on the newsstands in the United States. "Americans, this is an insult to the Star-Spangled banner. This is an insult to your own intelligence, and to every man who wears the uniform of the United States of America." He felt that all German newspapers should be shut down. "Wipe out the German-language press in the United States," he demanded. "Wipe out the German newspapers, and make this an America for Americans!"

Empey might not have realized how prophetic his words would become. Appeals such as these, for Americans to take justice into their own hands, were widespread in American periodicals at the time and had broad impact. Just a few weeks later, an article appeared in the September 14, 1918, issue of *The Nation*, a left-leaning weekly, which showed that Americans were indeed intervening when they heard people reading or speaking German in public. The article related the story of a naval officer who had snatched a German book from the hands of young woman in a crowded subway in New York. The officer publicly denounced the woman as a traitor for reading the German book and said there was "too much reading of pro-German literature." After issuing his reprimand, he ordered the woman to report to authorities an hour later to explain why she was reading such "traitorous" literature.

Thoroughly embarrassed, as *The Nation* explained, the woman reported to the customs office cited, with a coworker from the newspaper where she worked. Her colleague demanded to know why the officer had confiscated the book and why he had publicly lambasted her for reading a book by German diplomat Prince Karl Max Lichnowsky. The American government had circulated his book, *The Nation* noted, which was actually a harsh attack of Germany's bungled diplomacy that, it argued, was to blame for the start of the war. The naval officer then apologized. "To what avail" was the apology then, *The Nation* thundered. "This representative of the Naval Intelligence Bureau, who had never heard of Lichnowsky, continued to safeguard our liberties and prevent the poisoning of our minds," *The Nation* wrote in a caustic commentary.

The volume of attacks in the media grew louder after the United States' declaration of war. "The spy, the pacifist, the pro-German are carrying on their insidious, deadly drive in the city streets, the ranch house, in the Pullman," *McClures's* magazine published on April 4, 1918, in an article entitled "The Pull Together." "They are whispering their treachery in the big jobber's office and around the cast-iron stove of the general merchandise store at the corner. They are striving to break down our spirit, our morale, they are striving to drug us."

Another article, called "The German Octopus," was widely reprinted after first appearing in a magazine called *Living Age* on March 16, 1918. The article said that the "tentacles" of devious German-American activities reached into all parts of American life, that the nation was saturated with a network of German spies. Scores of other anti-German articles appeared in other periodicals at the time, when Imperial Germany's success on the battlefield was already frightening Americans. "Germany's Plots Exposed," "Use and Misuse of the Press," and "How the Germans Bamboozled the Public," were a few of the provocative titles.

Even violence against German-Americans was encouraged by the media. Popular cartoons appearing in such national publications as *Life, McCall's, The New York Evening World, The Chicago Daily News,* and *The Philadelphia Evening Ledger* frequently depicted obese German-American caricatures performing traitorous deeds or feigning support for the American flag while they were believed to be secretly harboring sympathies for Germany. *Life* magazine was especially caustic with its cartoons and its appeals for prompt vigilante action against "German-American traitors."

One cartoon in the October 11, 1917, issue of *Life* eerily foreshadowed the scene that would later be played out near Collinsville, Illinois, and in other towns across the country. In the cartoon (shown on page 88), a slim, strong American soldier who looks like Uncle Sam in a doughboys uniform was shown hanging a rotund, German newspaper editor from a tree branch. Entitled "Der Oudtlaw," a mangled term mixing the English word "outlaw" with a mock-German accent, the plump editor—with stereotypical German features, such as a thick, droopy blond mustache—was portrayed with a black mask over his eyes. He had a newspaper stuffed in his pocket with the masthead "last sedition"—a play on the words "last edition" and "sedition." Scattered on the ground beneath the hanging editor's feet were other German-language newspapers with distorted titles such as "Abendplot" instead of the German word for evening newspaper, Abendblatt, and the "Deutsche Pest" (German Plague) instead of the popular name for German-language newspapers of the era, Deutsche Post.

In the November 1, 1917, issue of *Life*, a cartoon called "A remedy for the soap-box traitor" (shown on page 26) was another illustration of such incendiary journalism. An archetypal German figure is portrayed standing on top of a soapbox giving a speech on pacifism, as suggested by a note sticking out of his pocket, bearing the word "pacifism." In the first frame, the German is standing on a soapbox beneath a street lamp, delivering his speech. In the second frame, a frowning American is seen climbing up the lamppost behind the German and dropping a noose around the neck of the oblivious speaker. In the third and final frame, the soapbox has been kicked out from beneath the German's feet, and the crowd, silent throughout the first two frames, is shown cheering wildly as the German, hanging from the lamppost, chokes in the noose.

The lamppost allusion is important, because it was first suggested by—of all people—the American ambassador to Berlin, James Gerard. In 1916, Gerard had responded to a warning made by the German foreign minister in Berlin that many Americans of German ancestry would rise up against U.S. entry into Germany's war against the British. The German minister had told Gerard that there were many Germans living in the United States who were ready to join the Irish to start a revolution if the United States entered the war on Britain's side. As Gerard later described it in a speech, "The

Foreign Minister of Germany once said to me 'Your country does not dare do anything against Germany, because we have in your country five hundred thousand German reservists [emigrants] who will rise in arms against your government if you dare to make a move against Germany.' Well, I told him that might be so but that we had five hundred thousand—and one—lampposts in this country, and that was where the reservists would be hanging the day after they tried to rise." Books were also published that further increased public doubt about German-Americans. *The German-American Plot: German Conspiracies in America*, by William Skaggs, was published in 1916, *The Enemy Within*, by John Price Jones in 1918, and *Fighting German Spies*, by French Strother in 1919.

Some of the most colorful anti-German books were written by former President Theodore Roosevelt, who probably did more than any other individual to fire up the rage against German-Americans. Roosevelt was a Republican president from 1901 to 1909, but later split with his party to form the Progressive Party, more popularly known as the Bull Moose Party. The former governor of New York led his Progressive Party to an uncommonly strong second-place finish in the 1912 presidential election, behind Woodrow Wilson but ahead of William Howard Taft, his erstwhile fellow Republican (leaving Taft with the dubious distinction of being the only incumbent president to end up in third place in an election).

Roosevelt was a larger-than-life character who had led a rough-and-tumble life as an explorer and naturalist in the West, after suffering from severe asthma as a child. Roosevelt was born into a wealthy New York family and moved west to become a rancher in the Dakotas in 1884. He later returned to New York and entered politics. He had agitated for the United States to go to war against Spain in what became the Spanish-American War in 1898. He fought in the ten-week war in Cuba himself, as a forty-year-old, with a group of wealthy Easterners and western cowboys called the "rough riders." When the United States finally declared war on Germany in 1917, Roosevelt's offer to organize a volunteer infantry division to fight the Germans was turned down.

Roosevelt had been urging the United States to join Britain in the fight against Germany for years, and he kept up a steady drumbeat of attack against German-Americans. He also railed against Wilson's neutrality policies, which he condemned, in a series of books. In 1916, he published a compilation of speeches—and magazine articles he had written for *Metropolitan* magazine—entitled *Fear God and Take Your Own Part*. Of German-Americans, Roosevelt wrote, "They play the part of the traitors, pure and simple. The hyphen is incompatible with patriotism." In addition, he reminded readers in his book of the number of ships sunk by "hideous Germans." Borrowing a line from the Spanish–American War that made him famous—"Remember the Alamo!"—Roosevelt enthusiastically implored his readers to "Remember the *Lusitania*!"

Earlier, Roosevelt had coined the term "hyphenate" to disparage immigrants who would not cast aside their ethnic attachments as soon as they should—which he thought should be when they arrived in the United States. Roosevelt was a prominent advocate of and partially responsible for a transformation in the way Americans viewed immigrant groups who tried to retain ties to their countries of ancestry. Before 1890, a hyphen to describe such ethnic group names as Irish-American, Italian-American, or German-American had been commonplace—a neutral or even positive description of the various ethnic groups. It was also a collective defense to the aggression the ethnic groups had encountered during the Nativist era of the mid-nineteenth century. But, as Luebke noted, hyphenism turned into something negative around the turn of the twentieth century, when it began to imply of a lack of loyalty to the United States.

Roosevelt's indefatigable campaign was a factor behind this palpable shift in attitudes. Roosevelt was not only against German-Americans retaining their ethnic loyalties and allegiances to their home countries, but also against Irish-Americans and other ethnic groups. But German-Americans were the biggest target at the turn of the century, and Roosevelt turned up the volume of his attacks on German-Americans once World War I began. In a speech in 1894, Roosevelt said that the United States had no need for German-Americans and wanted only "100 percent Americans." "Some Americans need hyphens in their names because only part of them have come over. But when the whole man has come over, heart and thought and all, the hyphen drops of its own weight out of his name."

Roosevelt kept the pressure up against German-Americans, writing, "There is no room in this country for hyphenated Americanism. When I refer to hyphenated Americans, I do not refer to naturalized Americans. A hyphenated American is not an American at all. Our allegiance must be to the United States. We must unsparingly condemn any man who holds any other allegiance. There is no such thing as a hyphenated American who is a good American." The former president became even more outspoken in his subsequent book, *The Focus of Our Household*, published in early 1917. "The Hun within our gates is the worst of the foes of our own household, whether he is pro-German or poses as a pacifist, or a peace-at-any-price man, matters little. He is the enemy of the United States." The derogatory term "Huns" to describe German soldiers was popularized by British propaganda. Kaiser Wilhelm II once used the word in a speech to German troops in 1900, as they were about to sail from Wilhelmshaven to China to help put down the Boxer Rebellion. The Kaiser told the troops to take no prisoners and urged them to fight as tenaciously and savagely as the Huns did a thousand years earlier. "A German should strike fear into the hearts so he'll be feared like the Hun." The deprecatory term would long haunt Germans.

Roosevelt maintained that the United States government was "knowingly allowing thousands of allies of Berlin to sow the seeds of treason and sedition in this country. The German-language papers carry on a consistent campaign in favor of Germany against England. They should be put out of existence for the war."

Roosevelt's disdain for the Germans might have had something to do with the fact that the former president was shot and wounded in a bizarre attack before a campaign speech in Milwaukee during the 1912 election by a deranged German-American saloon keeper named John Schrank. He shot Roosevelt from close range, but his .32-caliber bullet was slowed by the thick, fifty-page speech in the breast pocket of Roosevelt's heavy coat, as well as his steel eyeglasses case, but still managed to penetrate about three inches into his chest. Schrank was quickly arrested. Roosevelt was bleeding from the wound but he declined to go to the hospital, saying he wanted to deliver his speech first. He spoke for about ninety minutes and began his address by telling the audience, "Ladies and gentlemen, I don't know whether you fully understand that I have just been shot. But it takes more than that to kill a Bull Moose." He spent a week in the hospital after the speech. Because doctors said it would have been more dangerous to remove the bullet than to leave it in, it stayed lodged in the president's chest for the rest of his life.

Roosevelt never let up. In one colorful speech in New York in 1915, to a local chapter of the Knights of Columbus, Roosevelt said, "We must unsparingly condemn any man who holds any other allegiance. But if he is heartily and singly loyal to this Republic, then no matter where he was born, he is just as good an American as anyone else." Roosevelt warned that the United States would be in trouble if hyphenism prevailed. "The one absolutely certain way of bringing this nation to ruin, of preventing all possibility of continuing to be a nation at all, would be to permit it to become a tangle of squabbling nationalities, an intricate knot of German-Americans, Irish-Americans, English-Americans, French-Americans, Scandinavian-Americans or Italian-Americans, each preserving its separate nationality, each at heart feeling more sympathy with Europeans of that nationality than with the other citizens of the American Republic." Roosevelt said there was simply no room in the United States for hyphenated Americans. "The man who calls himself an American citizen and who yet shows by his actions that he is primarily the citizen of a foreign land plays a thoroughly mischievous part in the life of our body politic. He has no place here and the sooner he returns to the land in which he feels his real heart-allegiance, the better it will be for every good American."

DER OUDTLAW

A Life *caricature advocating the hanging of editors of German-language papers. Below: "The United States is cutting the German language out of schools"—and the Kaiser is shocked.*

A BODY BLOW

CHAPTER 6

HATE AND CENSORSHIP: THE END OF THE GERMAN PRESS

German culture in the United States was kept alive at the start of the twentieth century thanks in part to a flourishing German-language newspaper industry. German newspapers had an astonishingly wide reach and corresponding clout in parts of the country right up until the eve of World War I. In an era before television and radio, newspapers played a central role in keeping Americans informed, shaping the debate and influencing public opinion. It may be hard at times to fathom how much sway daily and weekly newspapers wielded a century ago, but they were indeed an essential part of many people's lives. In many American towns and cities, newsstands were crowded with foreign-language newspapers, serving not only German-American readers, but also immigrant groups from Italy, Russia, and France. There were also Yiddish newspapers. But due in part to the prominent role that the German press played, German-language newspapers became a lightning rod for the anti-German sentiment that was rising before and during the war.

Between the start of the war in 1914 and the events of early 1917 that triggered the United States' entry into the war, the German-language press in America was largely and unapologetically pro-German—leaving it exposed to criticism from increasingly enthusiastic American patriots eager to help fight the war at home. The highly visible German-language newspapers were tangible symbols of Germania on newsstands, doorsteps, businesses, and in the homes and hearts of many Americans. Some German-language newspapers were also renowned for a certain degree of arrogance in the way they upheld the German culture, or "Kultur," as Germans said, as somehow superior to American culture. This also made it easy for the American public, which began to look more closely and critically at the content of German newspapers, to turn against the German press as the hysteria against everything German gained momentum. "Of all the foreign-language newspapers, the German-Americans were the most critical of the American customs, the most arrogant in their attitude toward other minorities and the Anglo-Saxon majority," historian Carl Wittke wrote in *The German-Language Press in America.* He added that the German-language press encouraged its readers to believe that they were the "keystones of democracy" and to further the notion that German-Americans would play the leading roles in future generations, and that the United States would eventually be cast in a Germanic mold.

The reach of German-language newspapers before World War I was huge. There were 488 German-language daily and weekly newspapers in America in 1910, with a combined circulation of 3,391,000. But just ten years later, there were only 152 German-language publications still around. Their combined circulation plunged by sixty percent to 1,311,000, and by 1930 there were only ten German-language newspapers left. Fifty-four percent of all foreign-language papers in America in 1910 were German. By 1960, the share of German-language newspapers among the foreign-language press plunged to just seven percent.

It's not unusual for foreign-language newspapers associated with any ethnic group to eventually lose readers as a result of the forces of assimilation and the passage of time. Inevitably, many readers lose the ability or desire to continue to use foreign-language newspapers as a source of information. Yet the speed in which the German-language press all but disappeared between 1910 and 1920 is remarkable. In a decade when the number of other foreign-language publications of thirteen major ethnic groups increased, German-language papers were the only one to decline. From 1910 to 1920, the number of Spanish-language publications, for example, increased from twenty-one newspapers and 74,000 readers to thirty-three publications and 256,000 readers—while Yiddish increased from eight publications and 321,000 readers to twenty-three and 808,000. Italian-language newspapers also enjoyed strong growth in the decade, going from twenty-eight newspapers and 245,000 readers to forty newspapers and 584,000 readers.

The fate of daily newspapers during the decade of anti-German sentiment surrounding World War I is also illuminating. There were sixty-four German-language dailies in 1910, with a combined readership of 935,000. Before the dawn of radio, the daily newspaper was a crucial source of information for the masses. The evening newspaper was at the heart of turn-of-the-century society, a daily treat cherished by the various ethnic groups as much as by assimilated Americans.

Many of these German-language newspapers published, by and large, content similar to the English-language newspapers at the time, according to Wittke. The big exception was how they covered the war. "Eventually the only outstanding difference between the German and English newspapers published in the United States during the war was the almost complete absence of discussions of war practices in the German-language press," Wittke wrote. The alleged German atrocities in Belgium, which were getting wide coverage in American newspapers, were not mentioned at all or only in passing in German-language newspapers. "The German-language press refused to participate in this hysteria and as a result, at the end of the war, had no apologies to make and no lies to repudiate."

After the end of the war, there were just fourteen German-language dailies left and still doing business in 1920. They had a dwindling combined circulation of just 240,000, about a quarter of their level during their heyday just a few years earlier, before the war. The German daily press would never again come close to matching the scope and influence it had once wielded. By 1960, there were only four German-language dailies, with a total circulation of 74,000.

The forces of assimilation were accelerated by the war. Britain used its blockade of Germany during World War I to cut off the shipping of German periodicals into the United States. Because the mail going between Continental Europe and the United States had to pass through Britain as a result of the blockade, German periodicals containing the German side of the story often got no further than London, though there was no attempt to prevent readers of German publications in Britain from getting their copies. The British government effectively prevented German journals and newspapers from reaching Americans, which caused the editors of *The Nation* to complain. "The fundamental objection to the whole policy of excluding German publications is that it strikes another blow at intellectual foundations of democracy," *The Nation* published in an editorial on June 8, 1918. "If the American people are to think sanely and act wisely in the complicated and novel situations created by the war, they must be informed. Is there some convincing reason why English editors should be trusted while American editors should not?"

President Woodrow Wilson's administration moved to put limits on German newspapers, despite constitutional freedom-of-press guarantees, amid growing criticism about their continued publication after the United States entered the war. Wilson signed the Espionage Act on June 15, 1917, which made it a crime to interfere in any way with the war effort, a broad and loosely interpreted measure that was used as leverage against German newspapers. The postmaster general, a powerful figure at the time, was given the authority to ban any item from the mail "advocating or urging treason, insurrection or forcible resistance to any law of the United States," which was used to disrupt the publication and distribution of many German-language newspapers.

Wilson then signed another law, four months later, putting further restrictions on the German-language press. It was called the Trading with the Enemies Act of 1917, and was signed into law on October 6. Ostensibly designed to restrict trade with countries hostile to the United States, the law was also used by the postmaster general as a tool against the German-language press and against German-language book publishers that had built up flourishing businesses in a number of American cities before the war, especially Milwaukee, where the Germania Publishing Company was based. The law authorized censorship of all communications coming into or leaving the United States and allowed post offices, in the form of the local postmasters, to demand an English translation of newspaper or magazine articles printed in a foreign language. Newspapers could be exempted from the requirement after a period of a few months, provided they adequately displayed their patriotism. Indeed, many German-language newspapers were eventually spared the costly and time-consuming process. But a number of smaller newspapers could not afford the costs of translating their stories into English for the postmasters and had to fold. A few newspapers had their mail permits revoked by Postmaster General Albert Burleson, who interpreted the law as a veritable blank check to act as he saw fit to thwart the German-language press.

"This legislation sounded the death knell for scores of German-language newspapers operating on a marginal budget," Wittke noted. Those papers that managed to survive were forced to devote time and resources to translating articles into English. In order to circumvent the hassle and expense of the translating requirement and censorship pressure, there were thus soon fewer and fewer reports about the war in Europe. In effect, the law helped make the entire German-language press become trite.

German-language newspapers were torn, as the United States drifted toward war. Many had argued to keep the nation out of the war. Wittke's study of German-language newspapers revealed that most newspapers shifted their positions almost instantly after the Zimmermann telegram.

"The first few months after the declaration of war were by far the most important and perhaps most interesting in the history of the German-language press in the United States," Wittke wrote. "It was during these months that the editors performed mental gymnastics which finally landed them in their new positions of loyalty to the government and vigorous support of its war policies. The transition period was a period of terrible conflict of emotions in the hearts of many German-Americans, the tragedy of which many of their American neighbors failed to even sense, much less understand." Wittke added that by Summer 1917, practically all German-language newspapers had become "intensely loyal to the United States." The only exceptions, he noted, were the socialist newspapers, which maintained their opinion that the war was being fought for the benefit of capitalism.

Nevertheless, there were plenty of reasons for the growing resentment of the German press. The German newspapers had long served as a sort of collective community bulletin board and a point of reference for many German immigrants and Americans of German descent, bringing and holding together the diverse groups of German speakers around the country. German-language newspapers were a unifying force for many of those who came to the United States for an eclectic variety of reasons: religious freedom, to farm, to avoid conscription, and to search for prosperity. Second, the German press made itself vulnerable by campaigning so long and vociferously against American entry in the war.

Yet the question arises: Was the banishment of the German-language press warranted? There are two different schools of thought: some argued that German newspapers switched their positions in time, by and large supporting the American war effort, while others believe that the German press remained incorrigibly anti-American, even after the declaration of war.

Some of the most colorful and persuasive presentations of the sinister view of the German-language newspaper coverage came from a young Milwaukee journalist named Frank Perry Olds. Milwaukee was a leading center for German-language publishing houses, dating back to 1844. In Wisconsin, where many Germans had settled, there were nearly one hundred German-language newspapers. Olds published a series of articles in *The Milwaukee Journal*, starting on October 15, 1915, that portrayed the city's other daily newspaper, a German-language publication called the *Milwaukee Germania-Herold*, as unbendingly disloyal.

"Day in and day out, the *Milwaukee Germania-Herold* has preached division along the lines of race and other war prejudices," Olds wrote. "Day in and day out, it has endeavored to weld voters of

German descent into a powerful political weapon to be used by the National German-American Alliance and other representatives of Germany here. It has virtually without exception opposed the government of the United States in every step that President Wilson has taken to protect American sovereignty and the rights of American citizens against the aggressions of Germany," Olds continued, according to historian Richard O'Connor in *The German-Americans: An Informal History*, published in 1968.

Olds also published an article in the July 1917 issue of *The Atlantic Monthly*, one of the first U.S. magazines to accuse the German-language press of fomenting disloyalty. Shortly after Congress passed the Espionage Act, with its stiff penalties that could be imposed on anyone convicted of spreading false reports or statements with the intent to interfere with the success of the war effort, Olds wrote that the German-language press had remained loyal to Germany even after war was declared and disputed the claims of a switch to a pro-America bias by many German-American editors. He said that the German-language press had "not changed one iota" since the declaration of war.

"Though we knew that the German-Americans had steadfastly opposed the war between Germany and America, we thought that the actuality might convert them to a semblance of Americanism," Olds wrote in his *Atlantic Monthly* article. "It did not, but it made them more circumspect. Under the cloak of loyalty, they launched their new propaganda. Americans in general have been led to suppose that our pro-German press, once so emphatic in defense of Germany, is now supporting the United States in the prosecution of its war against the German empire. But nothing could be further from the truth. The pro-German press of the country has merely revised its propaganda to fit its present needs."

Olds helped the *Milwaukee Journal* win a Pulitzer Prize for meritorious public service, awarded a year later in 1919, because of its stand against Germany and his claims that German-American editors had continued to do their best to help Germany by "throwing stumbling blocks" in the way of the United States government.

Olds was convinced that the German-language newspapers

were still cheering for the wrong side, even after the United States entered the war in Europe. "At least one million men, women and children living in the United States are being misinformed and misguided," he concluded. "Many of them are, no doubt, being converted to the propagandists ways of thinking. The constitution allows them free speech. The constitution does not allow comfort to the enemy. The case of the German-American press is between the two. What are we going to do about it? What can we do about it?"

Herman Hagedorn, a Connecticut author and close friend of Theodore Roosevelt, was also especially caustic in his criticism of the German-language press. In *The Menace of the German Language Press*, Hagedorn said that Germans were dangerous. "They keep the heart soft at a time when the heart should harden itself against the sentimental call of the past so that the brain and the hand may better face the bitter exigencies of the present."

After an extensive examination of the German-language newspapers of the war years, Wittke came to a different conclusion: that the German-American newspapers had indeed undergone a metamorphosis in early 1917. Wittke quoted at length from prominent German newspapers of the era showing a clear pro-American stance as the United States moved toward war against Germany. Wittke tracked the events from the break in diplomatic relations in February 1917, when German ambassador Count Johann Heinrich von Bernstorff was told to leave the country.

Wittke quoted from an excerpt from the *Express und Westbote*, a leading German-American daily of the era, which had previously lobbied against entry into the war, showing the paper had done an about-face. "Our whole allegiance is to the United States—be she right or wrong," the newspaper wrote in a March 1917 editorial. "To the challenge sent, Woodrow Wilson could make but one answer—he has made it," the paper said about the president's decision to expel the German ambassador and break off diplomatic relations. "If the worst comes to worst, and war, with all its curse, falls upon this land—which we hope and pray will not be the case—the Americans of German birth or with German inclinations will be found standing shoulder to shoulder with those of other nationalities who have been made Americans in this, the great melting pot of the nations. Our country, may she ever be right—but our country above all, right or wrong."

Even though most German-language newspapers had made clear their support for the United States by April 1917, Wittke wrote that the transition had not been quick and complete enough to satisfy some Americans. In their eyes, it was a problem that some German-language newspapers continued to publish news stories about the war in a nonpartisan way: reports of German victories were not being covered as negatively as in other American newspapers, nor were Allied victories being sufficiently glorified. There were stories about German battle triumphs that did not include critical comments about the Germans, and for that they came under the microscope and were attacked as proof of a lingering "pro-German" attitude in the press.

German-American newspapers did change their tune, but they did not convert fast or furiously enough for some. Army enlistments in the Midwest, for example, were running well below the government's quotas, and even though support from Midwest and Western states for the United States to intervene in Europe's war had always lagged behind Eastern states, the German-language press was blamed because it had been so influential in parts of the Midwest. There had also been a perceptible lack of enthusiasm for Liberty Bonds in the Midwest and other parts of the country, and not only in those regions where the numbers of German-Americans were high.

By the summer of 1917, with the United States at war and conscription in place, the stage for the next level of hysteria against all things German was set. The German-language press was a massive target, despite the fact that most newspapers had already "strained every nerve to satisfy the patriotic critics," as Wittke wrote. In an attempt to demonstrate their patriotism, German-language newspapers began to include American flags in their mastheads. A century later, TV news anchormen were pressured to wear American flags on their lapels or risk being accused of lacking lacked patriotism, charges that sometimes had serious re-percussions for their careers.

Suddenly, German-language newspaper readers were being urged to memorize the United States' national anthem, and Ger-man newspaper editors were donating thousands of inches of column space to the government for free advertising of Liberty Bonds and other patriotic causes, in their belated and somewhat futile attempts to demonstrate their fealty to the United States. Too little, too late in the eyes of many Americans.

That the German-language press could even be allowed to continue publishing in the language of the enemy in the United States after the U.S. declaration of war against Germany was simply too much for some Americans. Writing in a 1918 pam-phlet entitled *America at War: A Handbook of Patriotic Education*, John William School argued that all who still continued to use German in their community or continued to read a German-language newspaper were disloyal. "How can persons become good American citizens when they refuse to employ the only means to that end, the English language?"

School singled out the German-language press for his sharp-est attacks, arguing that German newspapers should have died a natural death in the era after German immigration began slow-ing down in the 1890s. "There is a minority of our citizens of German extraction who deserve all the condemnation heaped upon them by their fellow citizens." School called these German communities in the United States derelict, and chastised such areas he called ethnically isolated for failing to properly assimi-late. "This community, served by its German-language newspa-per, knows no better, for its editor intentionally befuddles their intellects by his lies and poisons their judgment with his own malevolent venom."

The attacks on the German-language press seemed to gain momentum as the war continued. Some German-language newspaper editors who were German citizens were vilified and sometimes even interned as enemy aliens, along with thousands of other Germans living in America. The editor of the *St. Paul*

Volkszeitung, Fritz Bergmeier, was arrested in August, 1917, and sent to an internment camp in Georgia.

German-language newspaper editors sometimes received threatening letters, as did advertisers who continued to patronize the German press. The federal government also applied pressure on advertisers to stop supporting the German press. The United States Food Administration warned breweries in Milwaukee that unless they put an end to placing advertisements for their products in the German-language *Milwaukee Leader*, they might have trouble receiving allotments of malt, hops, and sugar, according to historian Frederick Luebke in *Bonds of Loyalty*.

Many Americans also felt a need to "do their own part" to support the war effort by taking steps against the German-language press. There were reports of rail workers, who had been delivering German newspapers for years, suddenly "erring" by throwing bundles of German-language newspapers off at the wrong stations, or of German-language newspapers mysteriously "disappearing" along the rail lines between stations. Even Boy Scouts in Cleveland took part in the action against German newspapers by "patriotically" burning German-language newspapers at public ceremonies. There were reports of school teachers sometimes discouraging their students from doing their part-time jobs delivering German newspapers. German-language newspaper editors were even spit on, Luebke wrote.

A local Home Guard defense organization in Hackensack, New Jersey—one of the myriad such groups that formed in that era to fight the war on the home front—even issued a ban on all German-language newspapers within city limits, on April 18, 1918. They forbade the city's news dealers from selling German-language newspapers. Unfortunately, only about a quarter of the large German-speaking community in Hackensack could understand English, but that did not matter to the Home Guard leaders.

The anti-German groups were especially outspoken in Iowa against the German-language press. Iowa county councils demanded that those newspapers be banned from the mail. The American Defense League circulated petitions urging President

Wilson to outlaw German-language newspapers entirely. And in Bloomington, Illinois, the *Bloomington Journal* was ordered to switch to an English-language format, even though the *Journal* was one of the oldest newspapers in the state.

The English-language press in the United States also played a role in accelerating the downfall of the German-language newspapers—in many towns and cities, they were in direct competition for many of the same readers. Understandably interested in increasing their own circulations at the expense of their German-language competitors, English-language newspapers sometimes portrayed their German rivals as havens for spies and traitors.

"Will somebody please tell us why a newspaper should be permitted to be printed in the German language anywhere within the border of the United States?" asked the *Philadelphia Inquirer* in a May 1918 editorial. "If it is an affront to teach German in the public schools—and it certainly is—is it not just as much of an affront to allow German-language newspapers to be circulated?"

Even stronger words could be found in the same May issue of *The Literary Digest,* from Richard Hurd, an executive at the American Defense Society: "There are about three hundred German newspapers in the United States. A majority of them are active centers of the German propaganda. It is folly and weakness not to immediately suppress these enemy publications."

Theodore Roosevelt was often in the headlines during the prewar months, with his attacks against German culture in the United States and especially against German newspapers. Even after the United States entered the war, Roosevelt continued to hammer away at a favorite theme. "We must have in this country one flag, and that is the American flag; only one language, the English language, the language of the Declaration of Independence, Washington's Farewell address, Lincoln's Gettysburg speech, and second inaugural; but one loyalty, that to the United States," Roosevelt told a group of workers at a munitions factory in Bridgeport, Connecticut, *The New York Times* reported on November 3, 1917. The former president also stressed the need to eliminate German-language newspapers, or at least force them to publish in English.

There were occasional appeals to reason. *The Literary Digest* conceded that millions of Americans would have no source of information if the German-language newspapers were outlawed. The magazine noted that many Americans could not understand any language other than German. "If the foreign-language press were discontinued tomorrow, the government would probably be obliged to restore it, unless willing to leave millions of loyal Americans in utter ignorance of what's going on about them," wrote Bernard Ritter, a journalist at the *New York Staats-Zeitung,* in an article reprinted in *The Literary Digest.*

The purge of the German-language press grew more intense in Fall 1917, when a fresh round of hysteria spread about German spies on the loose. "People believed and repeated absurd stories of German espionage," Luebke wrote. Many German-language newspaper offices were raided in September and October 1917 by authorities carrying orders from the Justice Department, and many such offices were targets for harassment from militants as well. In addition to pouring yellow paint on German newspaper offices, organizations such as the American Protective League broke into the offices of the *Chicago Arbeiter-Zeitung* and the *Sozial Demokraten,* as well as the *Philadelphia Tageblatt.* Files were indiscriminately confiscated, and some editors were arrested.

Considering the abuse and ostracism that German-language newspapers faced in the United States, it is easy to understand their decline in numbers and influence. That a group of ethnic-language newspapers could shrink from nearly one million daily readers to a quarter as many in just a few years looms as one of the darker episodes of American journalism in the twentieth century. Without the unifying force and cultural reinforcement of German-language news, German-Americans became more isolated in an increasingly frightening land.

War propaganda poster: German soldier depicted as gigantic, animalistic brute.

CHAPTER 7

WAR ON THE HUN DIALECT: NO GERMAN IN SCHOOLS

Surprising as it may seem today, German was by far the most popular foreign language in American schools before World War I. Taught in public schools in thirty-five states, it was the dominant foreign language learned in primary and secondary schools, as well as at universities. In states with large numbers of German-Americans, such as Texas, Missouri, Pennsylvania, Ohio, New York, and Wisconsin, German-language instruction often began as early as elementary school.

Before World War I, German-language teaching had been widespread in many regions of the United States, in large part a reflection of the millions of Germans who settled in those regions, but also because of the increasingly important role that Germany was playing in the worlds of science, education, music, culture, and commerce. In 1839, the Ohio state legislature even passed a law allowing school districts to establish entirely German-speaking schools in areas where an all-German school was desired by a certain percentage of parents. Cincinnati and Dayton soon set up such German-language schools—in which English was treated as just another subject—as well as bilingual schools, for which the city of Cincinnati became famous at the time.

Some other states, particularly across the Midwest, where many Germans had settled, adopted their own versions of the Ohio law. Thus, after 1840, the German language, which had already been taught in some parochial schools and in German-speaking communities, was being taught in public schools as well, in some cases almost exclusively, as Joshua A. Fishman explained in *Language Loyalty in the United States: The Maintenance and Perpetuation of the Non-English Mother Tongues*.

The affinity that the United States had for the German university system in the latter half of the nineteenth century also contributed to and deepened American attachment to the German language throughout U.S. school systems. Many of the leading scholarly periodicals of the era were printed in German, the top scientific journals were in German, and many American teachers studied at German universities. Between the Civil War and World War I, an estimated 10,000 Americans spent part of their academic studies at German universities abroad, as historian Richard O'Conner found. "In the United States all things German were particularly admired. The Germans knew how to make things work and that quality has always engaged the attention of the pragmatic American. German scholarship was increasingly imitated by American universities. Harvard adopted much from the German system." And as far as high schools were concerned, twenty-one percent of American high school students were taking German.

The popularity of German made it a large target for zealously patriotic Americans. And within three years, these figures were drastically reduced. This was mostly due to a campaign against the German language that began with World War I raging in Europe. They were carried out for the most part by two patriotic organizations, the National Security League, founded in 1914 and close to Woodrow Wilson, and its Republican spin-off American Defense Society, founded one year later. The honorary president of the American Defense Society was none other than former President Theodore Roosevelt.

The National Security League, rooted in the Democratic party, was headed by Solomon Menken, an Anglophile lawyer of Jewish descent, and Leonard Wood, a general whose ancestry went back to the *Mayflower* and who fought in the Apache wars against Geronimo. The League also had the support of London-born publisher George Putnam. The League's "Committee on Patriotism Through Education" gave directives to its 281 chapters scattered around the nation in all forty-eight states. The chapters were urged to use "all available means of local pressure to ban instruction of the German language," as *School and Society* wrote.

This process gained steam once the United States got involved in World War I in 1917. Members of the National Security League, who often held prominent positions in towns and cities nationwide, had notable success with the drive to remove German from schools. States began to write new laws that first restricted and eventually banned the teaching of German, first in elementary schools and then in secondary schools. Universities were not exempted from the campaign to do away with German instruction, despite the few scattered voices of reason trying to point out that, during a time of war, it might make more sense to study the language of the enemy rather than ban it.

But that sentiment was not widely shared. In a January 1918 pamphlet entitled "Throw Out the German and All Disloyal Teachers," the American Defense Society declared: "There is no longer one good reason why in American schools the German language should not be treated as Luxburg proposed for the ships of friendly Norway—'Spurlos versenkt'—sunk without a trace. We can make war on the Hun language, and we will. Any language which produces a people of ruthless conquistadors, such as now exists in Germany, is not fit to teach clean and pure American boys and girls, and the most ordinary principles of self-defense demand that it be eliminated." The reference to "Luxburg" was a controversy surrounding a German diplomat in Argentina, Count Karl von Luxburg. Luxburg proposed in a cable to Berlin that Argentine ships heading to Europe should be "sunk without a trace." The cable was intercepted, and American Secretary of State Robert Lansing made its contents public, which embarrassed Germany so much that Luxburg was dismissed.

Many towns and cities abolished the teaching of German in elementary schools even long before their states were able to pass bills into law. New York City, Philadelphia, Washington, D.C., Louisville, Jersey City, Hoboken, and Portland had all done away with German in their elementary schools by the fall of 1918. Also Cincinnati, Salt Lake City, Indianapolis, Duluth, Baltimore, and Long Beach were among the scores of cities in which German was banned from at least the elementary schools.

This was also due to the efforts of the Loyalty League of American Schools, a splinter group from the American Defense Society, that was organized in January 1918 with the principal aim of identifying "disloyal teachers" and having them removed from their classrooms. Its definition of "disloyal" meant any teacher who declined to go on the record in pledging allegiance to the United States. Teachers were forced to sign a statement affirming their loyalty, and those unwilling to publicly display their devotion to the United States were denounced. The Loyalty League adopted a platform stating that any teacher guilty of active or passive disloyalty should be immediately dismissed.

The League also promoted the formation of a "Junior Loyalty League," to be made up of students who would be on the watch for disloyal acts or statements from teachers or fellow students. But the League also looked beyond schools in its hunt for traitors. Most notably, it cast doubt on the loyalty of thousands of Americans suspected of harboring pro-German sentiments. Members were actively involved in writing letters to editors, in which they questioned the patriotism of universities, labor unions, and even churches.

The eradication of German-language instruction across the nation advanced at an alarming rate. According to information compiled by the National Bureau of Education in early 1918, there were only nineteen cities in the country with populations over 25,000—out of one hundred sixty-three—in which German was still being taught in elementary schools. Of the few cities in which foreign languages were still being taught, German was still the dominant language, with Italian and Polish being taught in elementary schools in just one city, and French and Spanish being taught in three cities. Otherwise, foreign-language instruction had been completely cut out of elementary schools by 1918.

The drive to completely eliminate German-language instruction from schools and universities was an ongoing process that
did not stop until after the armistice of November 1918 was
signed. And because German teachers felt compelled to be "mild
and non-combative," as described by Horace Peterson and Gilbert Fite in *Opponents of the War: 1917–18*, they never mounted
much of a defense, despite initial pleas to preserve foreign-
language instruction. While many educators might have initially
resisted cutting out German and language study because of the
war, the tide soon turned. Comments such as these from one
superintendent of schools in California were typical of the position taken by American school officials as the war progressed.
"I was in doubt before the war," the school official told *The New
York Times* on February 3, 1918. "I am becoming convinced now
that our public schools should teach one nation, one language,
one flag." The article concluded that "educators generally look
upon the teaching of foreign language in the lower elementary
grades as of very questionable value."

That view stood in contrast to earlier statements by some leading educators asserting how important it was to continue language instruction. Many had also tried to defend German specifically, arguing that the German language and the militarism of
Germany were two entirely different subjects that ought to be
kept separate. But this differentiated approach quickly fell out
of fashion as the war continued, and expressing such contrarian
views was even legally dangerous after the Espionage and Sedition Acts took effect.

Philander Claxton, the United States Commissioner of Education, told an audience at the Teachers College in New York City
on April 20, 1918, that even if Germany were to forever remain
an enemy, it would still be worthwhile to continue the study of
German. Claxton faced calls to resign from groups such as the
American Defense Society because of moderate views like that.
But he pointed out that it made even more sense to learn German
when the United States was at war. "England and France are pay-
ing more attention to the teaching of German than ever before,

and you can rest assured that the study of English is not being neglected in Germany today."

Claxton's assertions were supported by a 1918 article in a U.S. Office of Education journal called *School Life*, which reported that schools in Britain were not reducing their German study. Out of Britain's 1,049 schools at the time, three hundred eighty-seven offered German lessons in the 1911–12 school year, and in the 1917–18 school year, only eight fewer schools had German (379). The decrease, although slight, was attributed more to the "necessities of military service," which had depleted British schools of many teachers. "It does not appear that the war is responsible for any considerable decrease in the number of [British] schools including German in the curriculum," the government's education journal reported in its August–December 1918 issue.

The article also noted that many British educational journals, unlike their American counterparts, were actually calling for an increase in German instruction on account of the war. In the United States, however, efforts to rid schools of all German-language instruction continued largely unabated, usually under the guise of patriotism. City boards of education and town councils alike passed bans on the teaching of German and often required that classes in "patriotism" be substituted.

In New York City, home of the nation's largest school system and a flourishing German-American community, the board of education was becoming belatedly determined to crusade against German instruction, and because of its size, the purge of German from New York's school system served as an example for many other school boards across the country. The growing hostility toward the German language by New York City educators received considerable newspaper coverage in the spring of 1918.

The 1917-1918 school year began with the dismissal of three New York City teachers for "conduct unbecoming a teacher"—because they had remained neutral regarding the war—and ended in June 1918 with a blanket ban on German in New York City elementary schools. The board of education also insisted on cutting German instruction in New York high schools by eighty percent.

The three teachers were dismissed from DeWitt Clinton High School in November 1917, because they had, in the words of Board of Education president William G. Wilcox, "not shown enough enthusiastic patriotism for the war." New York State education commissioner Thomas E. Finegan later upheld the decision, declaring that a person "who does not without reservation utilize of all his intellectual powers and exert all his influence as a teacher to make the school a place where the fundamental principles of American philosophy of life and government are efficiently taught to properly support the Government in this war" has no business teaching in a New York school, according to a report in *The Nation* on November 19, 1918.

Despite the anti-German frenzy sweeping the school system, there were occasional voices of reason urging that German continue to be taught in New York public schools. They also warned of the perils of indiscriminate attacks on all things German. An article in *The New Republic* responded in strong language to a letter to the editor from a student expressing disappointment that there were faculty members of his high school German department who "insist on using the German language in preference to the English language for general intercourse." The student said that action should be taken against the teachers who continued to speak German while the United States was at war with Germany. "If no action can be taken by the city authorities, it is time for a patriotic committee to use tar and feathers—old fashioned, but very, very effective—in quest of satisfaction."

A liberal magazine launched in 1914, *The New Republic* advocated for U.S. entry into the war but objected to the dismissal of the three teachers in New York, observing that they had taught in that particular high school for twenty years and there was "never any question of their loyalty." The magazine advised its readers to be cautious of "those who are perverting our national cause into a bigoted and consciousness attack upon everything German," and also noted that these super patriots were "invariably creating"

107

a condition in which sedition thrives. The magazine added that Americans had a right to expect German-Americans to back the war effort against the Kaiser, which they were doing, and to support the United States, which it pointed out most had. However, readers were reminded that "we cannot ask him to war us the blood in his veins, to tear his tongue from his mouth."

New York dropped all German teaching in the elementary schools in December 1917, but the debate raged on regarding whether or not to abolish German from the city's high schools a well. The *Journal of Education*, which had followed the discussion in New York closely, noted there was pressure on the school board from the American Defense Society, which had its national headquarters in New York and was especially committed to eradicating German from all schools in the country's biggest city.

In March 1918, New York City school superintendent Gustave Straubenmuller ordered high schools to discontinue the use of nine German-language textbooks. Several reasons were cited for the ban, including the fact that they contained pictures of the ruling Hohenzollern family as well as the words and the music to the "Deutschlandlied," with its famous refrain "Deutschland über Alles." Other books banned by New York City schools had innocuous titles, such as *Fahrt nach Südwest* (Trip to the Southwest), *Deutsches Liederbuch* (German Songbook), and *First German Reader*. Evidently, inclusion of any favorable picture or painting of Kaiser Wilhelm (essentially any picture that did not show his deformed left arm), was enough justification to ban the book, according to a report in *The Literary Digest* on April 20, 1918.

While the spring 1918 debate raged on in the New York City school district about how much German to cut from metropolitan high schools for the following academic year, an editorial ran in *The New York Times* on April 5 urging that the German language and all German books be removed from schools. "For nearly three years it seemed as if the United States was to many of its citizens a province of the German Empire, and small provinces, cities, and villages of Prussia or Germany can still subsist in the United States," the editorial stated. "In many states these German dependencies, these Little Germanys, are found in language education and thought utterly German." *The New York Times* publisher at the time, Adolph Simon Ochs, was born to Bavarian parents who immigrated to the United States. Coincidentally, the editorial was published on the same day that Robert Prager was hanged by a mob in Illinois.

The American Defense Society had reason to cheer when the New York City Board of Education voted unanimously on May 29, 1918, for a resolution canceling introductory German courses in city high schools—at least for the duration of the war. The board cited several interesting reasons: aside from the usual charges that American teachers of German would "not have the proper enthusiasm" for it, or at least in theory "should not have" proper enthusiasm for the war against Germany, and that the loyalty of native German-speaking teachers was less than certain, the board further mentioned that after the war, "our trade with Germany will be vastly curtailed," and there was thus little worthwhile reason to continue the study of German.

"Even to compete in foreign trade with a Germany as strong as before the war (an improbable hypothesis), our export and import merchants need not know German," the school board observed in announcing the termination of introductory German courses. "Knowledge of German will not be necessary," the board said, according to a report in *School and Society* magazine on June 8, 1918. The Philadelphia Chamber of Commerce took a similar stance, arguing before the school board that there was no commercial value in the study of German in Philadelphia schools. "The use of the German language will be very much less important in the future than it ever has been, and speaking purely from this viewpoint, I feel that it should be eliminated from the courses of public schools, the high schools, and all kinds of schools," said Ernst Trigg, president of the Philadelphia Chamber of Commerce, according to a report in *The Milwaukee Journal* on April 14, 1918.

To the chagrin of the American Defense Society, German instruction was continued in some New York City high schools in the fall of 1918, though enrollment in German courses had fallen by some eighty percent when schools reopened. As it turned out, in light of the waxing animosity toward German, students were simply opting not to learn the language and that took away the pressure on the school board to issue an outright ban of German.

Though it was generally more difficult to enact statewide bans on German-language instruction, it was not impossible. According to an October 17, 1918, article in the *Journal of Education*, German instruction had been dropped completely from all schools in fourteen states, and similar laws to eliminate German from elementary schools were pending in sixteen other states. All states eventually passed laws concerning the German-language question, although in some cases the new laws did not take effect until after the war had ended. In Connecticut, for instance, the governor signed a proclamation barring the use of German "for instruction or purposes of administration in public or private schools" after July 1, 1917, the *Journal of Education* noted in October 1917.

The same was happening in Ohio. According to Ohio governor James M. Cox, the teaching of German was a "distinct menace to Americanism and part of a plot formed by the German government to make the school children loyal to it." Cox called in the Ohio state legislature for a special session and asked for a law that would abolish the teaching of German in Ohio elementary schools. The law passed, as did a similar law in Nebraska in November 1917. The most interesting example in that regard, however, is Wisconsin.

Wisconsin was home to many German-Americans who kept the language alive and thriving, in part through the schools. More than twenty-five percent of all high school students were learning German through the 1916–17 school year, according to the *Wisconsin Journal of Education*. There were a total of 11,209 pupils taking German in the state's 285 high schools.

In 1917, Wisconsin introduced legislation that suddenly put limits on German in the elementary schools. The new law in the

1917 Wisconsin State Statutes read, "All instruction shall be in the English language," and allowed instruction in foreign languages in classes only where the district board of education picked a "competent teacher." And it did not stop here. In its December 1917 issue, the *Wisconsin Journal of Education* urged that German be dropped from all schools "as quickly as possible" because a "deceived and outraged American people are finally awakening to the endless meshes of propaganda of an enemy nation regardless of the 'Kultur' or any other benefit which may result from the teaching of the German, and have decided to do away with a large part of that propaganda as represented in the teaching of the 'hun' dialect in our schools." The *Journal of Education* criticized the earlier policies of "practically compelling" every child to take German, claiming that such a requirement must have been planted by enemy propagandists. "But now it must stop. The schools of this country cannot be Americanized too soon."

As was the case in many other states, the teaching of German had already been stopped in most elementary schools in Wisconsin through action by local boards or because students had stopped taking German by the time the state acted and officially forbade its teaching in the elementary schools and restricted it in the high schools.

In Madison, as well as in many other Wisconsin cities, German-language offerings were completely dropped from elementary schools and cut back at the high school level as well. Of the fifteen German classes offered in Madison high schools before 1917, there were only two classes still being taught in the fall of 1918, according to Dave Mollenhoff in *Madison: A History of the Formative Years*. The scrapping of German from Madison high schools is particularly striking, considering that two-thirds of the city's population at that time was foreign-born and nearly half of those born abroad listed Germany as their country of origin. So about one-third of Madison residents were from Germany, yet the teaching of the German language was all but eliminated from their schools—with little protest or resistance.

Even the University of Wisconsin's German language department, the largest in America at the time and considered one of the country's leading departments, did not escape the anti-German hysteria unscathed. There were eight faculty members still teaching German by the end of World War I, and most were forced to assist in other departments to fill their schedules and "earn their salaries," as department chair Alexander Rudolph Hohlfeld described later in his 1948 book, *The Wisconsin Project*. Hohlfeld built up the department after arriving in Madison in 1901, according to research by Cora Lee Kluge of the University of Wisconsin German department. Under Hohlfeld, the department grew to become the largest in the nation. In the thirty-five years Hohlfeld served as chair, Wisconsin awarded eighty-eight PhDs in German. Hohlfeld also helped to establish a German House in Madison, believed to be the first residential foreign-language house at any American college or university. The German House had the misfortune of opening in summer 1914, just weeks after war broke out in Europe, and was forced to close in 1918 (although it was successfully reorganized in 1922).

In 1917, there were fourteen hundred students taking German courses at Madison—more than one-third of the university's four thousand students. But two years later, there were only 180 students still enrolled in German courses. The university still required students to take several years of foreign-language credits to graduate, but the German department grew unpopular due to anti-German sentiment during the war. Peer pressure and appeals to patriotism were successful in driving University of Wisconsin students away from German to study other languages. The French and Spanish departments—which until then had been dwarfed by German—grew rapidly, as Merle Curte and Vernon Carstensen noted in their 1949 report, *The University of Wisconsin: A History 1848–1925*.

Local pressure generated in the name of patriotism was also applied to the University of Wisconsin to curtail its German department. Richard Lloyd Jones, editor of the *Wisconsin State Journal* newspaper, argued that Wisconsin was the "most Germanized university in the West" and therefore in dire need of some

"Americanizing." Jones wrote that the German department in Madison was larger than the history, philosophy, and psychology departments, and pointed out that it was even larger than some of the school's basic science departments. Nearly ten percent of all Letters and Science credit hours earned at the University of Wisconsin in the semester before the war broke out were earned in the German department. That figure fell to about one percent by the end of the war. But despite the anti-German attitude sweeping the country, the University of Wisconsin's German department was not subjected to as much of a witch hunt, as other universities were. At the University Nebraska, for example, three professors were dismissed for not displaying enough patriotism.

In one incident that did occur at Wisconsin, a German professor got into trouble with university administrators after making a joke, deriding Liberty Loan buttons while speaking in the privacy of his office, as Wisconsin student Ernst E. Meyer later wrote in his 1930 autobiography, *Hey Yellowbacks!* The issue of Liberty Loan Bonds was a serious matter in the United States, in part because of their poor subscription rate in many areas of the country with high concentrations of Germans. Support for Liberty Bonds was a favorite method by which guardians of patriotism could gauge someone's loyalty. "He was speaking to a colleague; there was no one else in the room," Meyer wrote, who was later expelled by the University of Wisconsin and spent a year in jail for being a conscientious objector during the war. "The colleague, his pretended friend, carried the jest in outrage to the university authorities. The professor was expelled, with wide publicity. The newspapers branded him a spy."

Under pressure for its pro-German reputation, the University of Wisconsin administration also tried to show its patriotism by stripping away an honorary degree it had awarded to the German ambassador to the United States, Count Johann von Bernstorff, in 1910. The University of Pittsburgh had also awarded an honorary doctorate to Bernstorff that year, who was a colorful and high-profile figure in the United States before he was expelled in 1917. Wisconsin was under pressure in 1917 to prove that it was not a "Germanized" university, especially after a controversial visit by Princeton University professor Robert McElroy, who was upset about a perceived lack of patriotism exhibited by a group of Wisconsin cadet corps students during a long speech he gave in a cold, damp meeting hall.

Not only did the University of Wisconsin's German department come through the war relatively well, it also recovered quickly afterward. By 1927, enrollments had climbed back up to prewar levels. One explanation for why Wisconsin's German department proved to be resilient was because of the prestige it enjoyed in Madison and beyond the state's borders, thanks in part to the efforts of Hohlfeld. Another reason for the department's rapid return to prewar enrollment levels was Hohlfeld's 1920 addition of courses that examined German literature in English translation. Worried by low postwar enrollment in German courses and the unpopularity of reading German literature at the time, he pragmatically offered the first literature-in-translation course. The courses also benefited underemployed German professors, whose livelihoods were jeopardized by low enrollment and the anti-German fever.

The German department at Iowa Wesleyan College in Mount Pleasant, Iowa, did not fare as well. The Board of Trustees there voted on April 19, 1918, to abolish German-language instruction. There was a large German community in the area, and six of the college's professors had been born in Germany. But that was not enough; *The Milwaukee Journal* reported from the meeting that the head of the German department himself had recommended dropping German.

Yet merely dropping German-language classes was not enough for some super patriots, who also wanted to see German textbooks destroyed. After the South Dakota Council of Defense ordered an immediate halt to German instruction in all state schools in February 1918, including the universities, seventy-five students broke into the local high school in Yankton, removed all of the German books, and threw them into the Missouri River. North Dakota eliminated German instruction entirely from public schools shortly thereafter, as did countless other cities and towns across the nation.

Throughout the debate on German-language instruction in the United States during the volatile years of World War I, the *Journal of Education* drew comparisons of attitudes from many educators. The journal's progression from defending German instruction to tormented ambivalence and ultimately to advocating the expulsion of the German language from schools serves as a barometer for the entire era, as educators and school boards moved through similar phases, ranging from support for German at the outset to ultimately abandoning it. Because of this, the *Journal of Education*'s shifting stance on German is worth a closer look.

During the United States' neutrality years and even into the opening months of America's involvement in the war, the Boston-based journal urged tolerance and moderation in dealing with German-language instruction. Even in the face of growing anti-German sentiment, the magazine urged readers to distinguish between Germany and the German language, insisting that the language of Goethe, Schiller, Beethoven, and Bach not be lumped together with Imperial Germany's militarism. It tried at first to counter the arguments that German was the language of "the Hun" and that appreciating German culture was disloyal or unpatriotic.

But these initial appeals fell on deaf—or frightened—ears. As the sentiment against all things German and German-language instruction gained momentum across the country in the spring of 1918, the *Journal of Education* was evidently feeling the pressure and began to waver. As late as February 17, 1918, the *Journal* had published an editorial reflecting the times, arguing on behalf of keeping German in the schools but also bowing to the inevitable pressure from the patriotic groups. "We do not think the teaching of German can be in any ways harmful to American students, and we wish it might not be made a patriotic issue. But if made a patriotic issue, if pro-German or other anti-American groups make a fight for its retention, and if its retention can then be construed as a triumph for the enemy within our borders, then German should be promptly and emphatically eliminated."

By April 25, 1918, the *Journal of Education* noted with a sense of resignation that there was little that could be done to prevent the complete eradication of German-language instruction in United States schools if that is what the majority of Americans wanted. The *Journal* recounted a recent address by Nebraska governor Ross Hammond, who had enthralled an audience with a speech in which he said, "There must be no teaching of a foreign tongue in our schools, and no paper printed in a foreign language should be allowed in the United States mail."

Noting the "wild" cheers the speech elicited, the *Journal of Education* commented, "It is all well enough to say that we are not fighting the German language, but the fact remains that any audience where it has been tested out will cheer an attack on the German language more wildly than any other phase of a patriotic address . . . arguments signify little when the great mass of people have such convictions."

By July 1918, the *Journal* had given up completely, joined the bandwagon, and denounced the use of German in any form. "It is undeniable that all traitorous tricksters champion the use of German in schools and elsewhere . . . It does not seem necessary to try . . . protecting the use of a language which is more serviceable to traitors than to patriots." The *Journal* concluded that "only one hundred percent Americans always use English and that there is absolutely no defense for using the German language in schools."

In October 1918, as the war in Europe was nearing its conclusion, the *Journal of Education* gleefully predicted the worldwide demise of the German language as well as German influence. "German threatens to become a dead language in this country, and with none of the respect that the educational world, at least, has for the ancient language commonly called 'dead.'"

By the time the storm had passed and the war ended in 1918, the aim of the American Defense Society had been accomplished: foreign-language instruction in general, but especially German, had been greatly reduced in American schools. War-time hysteria had succeeded in eliminating German from most public high schools, and nearly eradicated German entirely from elementary schools by the end of the war. Throughout this wide-scale assault on the German language, many Americans of German ancestry faced a paradoxical situation: if they openly displayed loyalty to the United States, they ran the risk of being accused of feigning patriotism and being persecuted for that. Yet if they did not overtly display their loyalty, they risked being denounced and persecuted as traitors. It was an unenviable position to be in, and attacks from school administrators, anti-German organizations, and mainstream newspapers made the situation all the more unbearable. By the end of the campaign to end German-language instruction, another aspect of German culture in America was significantly diminished, and members of the German-American community were even more isolated.

During the height of anti-German hysteria, dachshunds were killed.

CHAPTER 8

LIBERTY CABBAGE AND SLAUGHTERED DACHSHUNDS

During World War I, patriotism soared to what, in hindsight, seemed like absurd levels. As if it would help the United States win the war in Europe, Americans purged German terms from restaurant menus, maps, animal names, and even illnesses. Hamburgers were turned into "liberty sandwiches" or "liberty steaks," and German measles were renamed "liberty measles." A popular, early-twentieth-century doughnut-like treat filled with cream and jelly, known as the Bismarck pastry, was renamed "American beauty."

There seemed to be no limit to how far patriotic Americans were willing to go to eradicate all traces of German in the United States. Dachshunds were renamed "liberty hounds" or sometimes called "liberty pups." There were even reports of mad attacks carried out in the name of patriotism: some dachshunds were stoned to death because of the breed's German name. In Columbus, Ohio, German canine breeds such as German shepherds and dachshunds were taken from their owners and slaughtered.

Removing German-sounding names as a demonstration of patriotism might seem like a cosmetic change, but the Americanization of German town and street names was symptomatic of a deeper level of prevailing hostility. During World War I, some extremely patriotic Americans campaigned tirelessly to strip as much of the Germanic influence as possible from the United States, and in their eyes, that meant Americanizing as many German names as possible. They had an ally in the government in a new agency called the United States Committee on Public Information (CPI). Created by the Wilson Administration when the United States declared war on Germany, the CPI was set up to influence public opinion and rally support for America's participation in the war, a genuine concern, considering the earlier antiwar sentiment prevalent in some parts of the country. The CPI was also called "Creel Committee," after its chairman, George Creel, a journalist from Missouri who had previously written and drawn for the papers of William Randolph Hearst and Joseph Pulitzer. Creel, a Democrat, had also worked on Wilson's reelection campaign. The CPI employed hundreds of artists, journalists, and public relations people, among them Edward Bernays, who is widely regarded as the father of modern PR, but also 75,000 volunteers. It fed news stories about the glorious American war effort to American newspapers, distributed anti-German posters depicting German soldiers as huns, and even dabbled in war documentaries, namely *Pershing's Crusaders, America's Answer (to the Hun)*, and *Under Four Flags*.

One of the issues Creel's organization worked on was to Americanize German names. They were coming up with new terms such as "liberty cabbage" for "sauerkraut." But the CPI did much more than that. Its aim was to stifle controversial opinions about the war, because the government did not want—and could ill afford—a public debate on the merits of its entry into the war overseas. The CPI encouraged authorities to clamp down on anyone who did anything that could be seen as counteracting the government's goal of winning the war.

Working hand in hand with Creel was the American Defense Society, with the stated aim of making German a "dead language." The society pushed its campaign to eliminate all German names. "Turnvereine" became "Gymnastic clubs," "German" banks became "American" banks, the Germania Life Insurance Company became "National Guardian Life Insurance," the "Deutsches Haus" in Indianapolis became the "Athenaeum," and "Germania" hotels became known as "American" hotels. Clerks in state offices sometimes even refused to pick up pencils with the words "Made in Germany" printed on them. There was also a proposal to eliminate use of the Fahrenheit temperature scale because of the German origin of the term with Celsius (this was obviously never implemented, much to the chagrin of visitors today from around the world). There was also a discussion on discontinuing use of the word "kindergarten" in the U.S. because it was a German word, though some of the first kindergartens originated in Switzerland.

Many towns, cities, and people Americanized their names. The American Defense Society was again at the forefront of the campaign to remove German names from cities, streets, and squares. In a letter distributed to its three hundred branch organizations, the American Defense Society urged all regional members to exert pressure on their local authorities to get German names removed and to replace them, for instance, with the names of French and Belgian towns that had been battered or destroyed by the war.

"It is interesting to note to what extent towns in the United States bear German names," said Richard Hurd, chairman of the American Defense Society, in a report in *The New York Times* in 1918. "There are almost as many American cities named Bismarck as are named after our own great Lincoln. Hamburg has a namesake in twenty of our states. Eight cities are named Bremen, eleven Dresden, and there are twenty-two Hanovers. The Germans who came to this country years ago doubtless brought with them pleasant recollections which they sought to perpetuate in these names. Such associations can no longer exist."

The American Defense Society's appeal to remove German names was a resounding success. Many more streets, parks, and schools were renamed than towns or cities, but there were still plenty of examples of towns changing their names. Germantown, Nebraska, was renamed Garland, after a local soldier killed in action in Europe. Berlin, Iowa, became Lincoln, Iowa, and Berlin, Michigan, was changed to Marne—named after the second battle of the Marne in World War I. East Germantown, Indiana, became Pershing. Luxembourg, Missouri, was renamed Lemay. The farming town of New Brandenburg, Texas, was changed to Old Glory, and Marienfeld was given the new name of Stanton. Houston's German Cemetery was renamed Washington Cemetery.

Countless street names were changed across the country as well. In Cincinnati, which had a large German-American community, German Street became English Street, Berlin Street was turned into Woodrow, Bismarck became Montreal Street, Bremen renamed Republic, Frankfort was switched to Connecticut Avenue, Hanover to Yukon, Hapsburg to Merrimac, Schumann to Meredith, Vienna to Panama, Humboldt to Taft, and Hamburg became Stonewall. The city's German National Bank was renamed Lincoln National. In Buffalo, where about a third of the population was German-American, the German-American bank changed its name to Liberty Bank. In New Orleans, Berlin Street was renamed Pershing, while Chicago saw Lubeck, Frankfort, and Hamburg Streets Americanized as Dickens, Charleston, and Shakespeare. Chicago also renamed its prestigious German Hospital as Grant Hospital.

Wisconsin's state legislature was especially eager to demonstrate its patriotism and passed a law in 1917 to expedite the process for towns and cities that wanted to change their names. Under the new rules, a city or town needed only a simple majority of eligible voters to sign a petition declaring the desire to rename the town. Approval by a local common council was all that was required beyond the petition. Only one town in the state changed its name, though: Schleisingerville, Wisconsin, was named after its founder in 1857, State Senator Baruch Schleisinger Weil, but it became "Slinger" in 1917. The state of Wisconsin also made it much easier for residents to Americanize their family names and even provided new legislation enabling minors to change their names on their own. "Any resident of this state, whether a minor or of full age, may, upon petition of the circuit court of the county where he resides . . . have his name changed," the new law stated.

Many schools nationwide also got swept up in the spirit of removing as many German remnants of their heritage as possible, by altering, Anglicizing, or completely changing their names. Chicago's Bismarck School became General Frederick Funston School.

Manifestations of American Defense Society diatribes against German names could be seen at local levels across the country. The January 12, 1918, *Wisconsin State Journal* published a letter to the editor in which the writer expressed his dismay that the German-American Bank across the street from the state capitol had not yet changed its name. "Our love for America should not tolerate anything which is German being ahead of anything which is American and we will not tolerate it," the writer complained. "The German-American Bank should be forced to discontinue business until its company chooses a name which is thoroughly American, purely Democratic, and 'patriotic.'" The bank was soon renamed the American Exchange Bank. The German Exchange Bank of New York changed its name to the Commercial Exchange Bank on January 8, 1918. In 1917, the Germania Life Insurance Building in St. Paul was renamed the Guardian Building. An enormous statue of the company's symbol, the Germania figure, could not be disguised or hidden, so it was taken down.

But it was not only German names that were being removed en masse. The contempt for other symbols of Germany grew intense. Amid rumors across the country that German saboteurs were on the loose, Americans felt compelled to stand up and take action. Some of the incidents were simply bizarre with wildly patriotic Americans going berserk at times in their quest to destroy or attack anything with even a remote connection to Germany.

In Eugene, Oregon, a piano belonging to a German singing society was destroyed. In Green Bay, Wisconsin, a group called the Loyal Knights destroyed a statue that decorated a building on North Washington Avenue during the night of April 10, 1918. The Knights claimed that it was a statue of Germania. But its owner, a former congressman named Gustav Kustermann, tried to convince the Knights that it was actually a statue of the goddess Liberty. He said that the statue had thirteen stars on its emblem—each representing the original thirteen states to join the union—and tried to convince them that should serve as proof that it was American and not German. Kustermann lost the argument. The statue was pried away from its second-story perch and smashed to bits. Making matters worse, when Germania hit the ground, it demolished two display signs and a large window, as *The Milwaukee Journal* noted on April 11, 1918.

A Davenport, Iowa, man named E. J. Kelly got so worked up about the Germans while watching a movie "showing German atrocities" at a screening on April 7, 1918, that when an image of the Kaiser appeared on the screen, he leaped up suddenly from his seat and shouted, "If I can't get you over there, I'll get you over here." Kelly took a revolver out of his pocket and "shot" the Kaiser on the screen, according to a front-page report in *The Milwaukee Journal* on the following day. "The bullets pierced the Kaiser's left lung . . . The screen was wrecked. Kelly was not prosecuted."

In Washington, D.C., a bronze statue of Frederick the Great, which had stood on the banks of the Potomac River for decades, was removed by order of President Woodrow Wilson, as noted in a report in *The Milwaukee Journal* on April 11, 1918.

The animosity against all things German frayed the fabric of American society and destroyed bonds that had been forming in the United States even prior to the 1776 signing of the Declaration of Independence. The Pennsylvania German Society, for example, was founded in 1763 and had been a respected institution for more than a century. But it had to cancel its popular German Day festivities once America entered the World War I, putting an abrupt end to a one-hundred-fifty-year tradition. Other ethnic German celebrations, such as an annual singing festival in Germantown, Kansas, were also scrapped forever in 1917. "Throughout the nation, German-American organizations whose loyalty had never been questioned found it advisable to suspend all activities," Wittke wrote.

"The war precipitated a violent, hysterical, concerted movement to eradicate everything German from American civilization," according to Wittke. "It was led by a minority of extremists, but a large part of the American population participated in the patriotic 'drive against Teutonism.' . . . German-Americans suddenly suffered from the hatred and persecution of a large number of their fellow Americans with whom they had once lived in harmony, good neighborliness, and mutual respect."

CHAPTER 9

BANNING BEETHOVEN: THE HOWL OF THE CAVE MAN

The all-out war on German influence in the United States only grew worse as the war dragged on and soon it encompassed all aspects of German-American society, making it increasingly difficult to be German in America.

In May 1918, Iowa governor William L. Harding issued a proclamation placing a blanket ban on the use of all foreign languages, an executive order known as the "Babel Proclamation" that was aimed primarily at the German speakers in his state. The order stated that English was the only language permitted in public in Iowa and that foreign languages were banned from all train cars, telephone conversations, public addresses, in public and private schools, and in churches.

The Council of Defense pushed for the introduction of a similar ban in South Dakota, Iowa's neighbor to the northwest, prohibiting the use of German in sermons, in public schools, and over telephone lines. The ban was especially problematic for older Germans, some of whom had never become proficient in English, and for many other immigrant groups as well, including Scandinavians living in states such as Iowa, Minnesota, and South Dakota. Many communities were forced to put an end to public meetings, because too few understood English or had any interest in learning it.

The laws against foreign-language use during that wartime frenzy were strictly enforced, and many ordinary Americans were eager to do their part to protect the nation's security by informing local authorities about people who violated the ban. In Iowa's Le Claire

Township, four women were fined a total of $225—a considerable sum in 1917—for speaking in German on the phone.

This posed special problems for churches whose services were in German. The tradition of German-language church services throughout the Midwest and parts of the West had been a vehicle of communication that brought together German speakers in pockets of the United States for more than a century. Throughout the 1800s and into the first two decades of the 1900s, church services played an important role for many people in retaining their language and neutralizing the forces of assimilation. Outposts of German language and culture, churches in towns scattered across the Midwest continued to use German, in many places exclusively, right up until the war. Now, some churches abandoned services in German and Scandinavian languages altogether for the duration of the war. Other churches closed entirely. If, as occasionally happened, a minister dared to continue preaching in German, he ran the risk of being reported to the state defense council or being beaten by vigilantes.

Maintaining German in churches was not necessarily a conscious or coordinated effort on the part of German-Americans in the United States to preserve their language and extend their cultural influence across the country. Instead, there were more pragmatic reasons for the prolonged popularity of German-language church services: for many parish members, German was the only language they understood. Indeed, many Germans arrived in the United States precisely for that reason—the pursuit of religious freedom. The majority of German immigrants were Lutheran or Catholic, but there were also smaller groups, such as the Mennonites and Amish, who migrated to areas of the Midwest in the pursuit of religious freedom. The first Mennonites and Amish settled in Pennsylvania as early as the early 1700s.

In addition, the Mennonites were deeply committed to pacifism. They stood out among the colonialists during the Revolutionary War because of their opposition to fighting for the country's independence from Britain. Later waves of Mennonite immigrants settled farther west, in Ohio, Illinois, Indiana, Iowa, and Missouri.

Their opposition to war had also rankled American patriots during the Civil War era, and continued as the Great War began.

When war broke out in Europe in 1914, many German church-es had initially refrained from supporting either side. Oblivious to many of the nation's other most pressing issues, many Ger-man-Americans in the myriad small towns across the country pre-ferred to remain blissfully unaware of the war developments in Europe. "For most leaders of the German-American churches," Frederick Luebke wrote *Bonds of Loyalty*, "the European war was not a subject calling for partisan comment. The churches as eth-nic institutions had no interest in a German victory compared to their concern for the unhampered maintenance of the German language and culture."

There were certainly plenty of supporters of Germany among the clergy in the United States during the prewar years. But they tended to act as individuals rather than as representatives of an entire ecclesiastical body. And they were by no means a majority. As the United States drifted toward war against Germany, espe-cially after the *Lusitania* was sunk, and as their culture and lan-guage came under attack, many churches finally reacted and made their allegiance to the United States clear. Their very means of communication was under threat as the winds of war picked up and their entire order was suddenly in jeopardy. "How could they not respond?" Luebke asked.

Even though they had an enormous reach into their communi-ties in some parts of the United States, German-language churches had already been facing a gradual decline in membership and influ-ence since well before the outbreak of the war. Some churches, es-pecially those in areas near major towns and cities, saw their mem-bership and support wane as a result of declining levels of German immigration after the peak in 1892. Some churches adapted to the changing situation by offering some sermons in English.

Hermann, Missouri, is one such place that was moving with the times, albeit slowly. Hermann was settled in the 1830s and its population soon swelled with idealistic "Forty-Eighters" who had fled German-speaking parts of Central Europe after the failed

cf. Hermann statue in New Ulm

revolution of 1848. The town was named after Hermann der Cherusker, a warrior who led the defeat of the Roman Empire in the year 9 A.D. at the Battle of Teutoburg Forest. The town was founded by an organization called the Deutsche Ansiedlungs-Gesellschaft zu Pennsylvania, which wanted to perpetuate German cultural traditions. German was indeed still being spoken almost exclusively in many of the towns along the Missouri River right up into the twentieth century. Irish immigrants and freed slaves who settled in the town in the years after the Civil War ended up learning German to communicate with people in town because English was not the first language used.

The effects of assimilation were being felt more acutely in the first decade of the twentieth century. In 1907, when a new Lutheran church was being built in Hermann, the pastor delivered his address in English. In 1910, it was decided that one English service per month should be held for the benefit of younger members of the church, who were either unable to understand German or less interested in continuing to use the language of their parents and grandparents. Hermann church leaders feared that their church would lose its younger members, who tended to be more open to the forces of assimilation, if it continued to rely solely on German, according to John Hawgood in *The Tragedy of German America*. So even though the looming war against Germany would accomplish in just a few short months what might have taken decades under other circumstances, the fabric of German-American society in the United States was already starting to unravel in some regions well before 1917.

The news that the United States had entered the war in Europe on the side fighting against Germany nevertheless came as a great shock to many German-American church leaders. A German Lutheran pastor in a small Texas town was in the middle of his sermon when he was handed a note with the news that America had declared war on Germany. The pastor was so stunned that he was unable to continue speaking. There were also reports of suicides committed in draft camps by German-American recruits who were disturbed that they were bound for Europe to fight their blood relatives, Hawgood wrote. As the levels of wartime hysteria rose in the United States in 1918, the continued use of the German language in churches made them a popular target for scrutiny and attacks by zealous American patriots. Many states followed the pattern established in South Dakota and Iowa, which banned German from church services. In some midwestern towns, ministers caught speaking German were forced either to switch to English or be run out of town, and there were numerous reports of ministers being tarred and feathered.

There were incidents of pacifist ministers being persecuted and imprisoned as well as abused or threatened for making even mild statements against the war —incidents that showed how the "Espionage and Sedition Acts" encroached upon freedom of speech during the war era. The case of the Reverend David Gerdes of Rockford, Illinois, was especially enlightening.

Gerdes was accused of urging his followers not to buy Liberty Bonds and had allegedly said that purchasing Liberty Bonds would be tantamount to firing bullets at Germans. When his case finally came to trial after the war had ended, the judge presiding, K. M. Landis, asked Gerdes what he would "do if a Hun were attacking the honor of his daughter?" Gerdes replied that he would plead in God's name that his daughter be spared, but insisted that he would not kill the man, even though the man was a brute. "Take them out of the court," the judge shouted to the bailiff. He then sentenced Gerdes to ten years in Leavenworth prison, though his sentence was later commuted and Gerdes ended up serving only one year in jail, according to Horace Peterson and Gilbert Fite in *Opponents of the War: 1917-18*. Also in Lowden, Iowa, the pastor of a German Evangelical Church was charged with treason, even though his son was in the U.S. Army. A mob threatened to hang him unless he promised to hang an American flag from his pulpit.

Reinhold Niebuhr, an American-born Lutheran theologian who later became a leading voice of liberal conscience throughout the United States in the 1950s and 1960s, grew up in a German-speaking family in Missouri. In 1917, he was a twenty-four-year-old pastor of a German-speaking congregation in Detroit when

German-Americans came under general suspicion of having divided loyalties. Despite being a pacifist, Niebuhr urged German-Americans to show their patriotism for the United States, and his ardent appeals for Germans to show their loyalty to the United States put him in the national spotlight for the first time.

One of the final bastions of German culture to come under attack was music. Until 1917, German music had largely been immune to the attacks on German-speaking society in the United states. German immigrants brought with them to the United States all kinds of musical traditions—choral, brass, string, and sacred music. In many American cities, it was the German immigrant community that was at the center of musical culture, with bands, operas, symphonies, and choral societies.

But ultra-patriots in the United States felt threatened by German music and felt compelled to protect Americans from the "contamination" coming from music by purging the nation of classic German and Austrian composers such as Ludwig van Beethoven, Johann Sebastian Bach, and Wolfgang Amadeus Mozart, beginning with community orchestras. Some also worked to have the conductors of the orchestras interned as enemy aliens if they were of German origin. The music of Beethoven came under special scrutiny, and symphony orchestras in the United States either voluntarily dropped Beethoven and other legendary German composers from their repertoire or were forced to drop them.

W. J. Henderson, a music critic for *The New York Times*, noted that in the spring of 1918, the music of Beethoven, Schumann, and Bach was suddenly being called into question after having gotten through the early years of the war relatively unscathed. In an article for *The Literary Digest*, Henderson wrote, "Last autumn there was almost no opposition to the singing of songs in German. The present writer attended numerous concerts at which 'lieder' of the familiar masters, Schumann, Schubert, Brahms, and Beethoven, were heard and apparently with satisfaction by audiences of considerable number."

Henderson went on to explain that "it is beyond the power

of the printed word to exaggerate the feelings of resentment" he was feeling toward the German singers, musicians, and their language at that point, just six months later, in the spring of 1918. He counseled his readers not to resist the rising tide against German music and opera. He told music lovers to take a new look at Italian, French, and Russian composers. Put German on the shelf, Henderson urged, at least until the war was over. "The lovers of music must do without the compositions of living Germans and the songs of any Germans with the original text until the world has purged itself of its present fever."

In June 1918, the *Los Angeles Times* used extraordinarily colorful language to assail German music, arguing that German music must be barred entirely after an earlier decree banned German music in the schools. "German music, as a whole, is dangerous, in that it preaches the same philosophy, or rather sophistry, as most of the German literature. It is the music of conquest, the music of the storm, of disorder and devastation. It is symbolical of neither the sunbeams singing among the daisies, nor of grand cathedral bells calling worshippers to prayer. It is rather a combination of the howl of the cave man and the roaring of the north winds."

Some well-known German conductors living in the United States and running popular orchestras were caught off guard by the declaration of war. Many were fired because they were German, and some were sent to the internment camps set up for German aliens—a dark forgotten chapter of American history. One of those was Frederick A. Stock, the German conductor of the Chicago Symphony. He was fired, as was the conductor of the Boston Symphony, Karl Muck. He was also harassed by audience members at concerts for including works by German composers, despite warnings to drop them. Muck even faced two federal investigations into "suspicious activity" and was arrested in 1918 and interned as a "dangerous enemy alien" in Georgia—along with twenty-nine members of his orchestra. The interned orchestra kept busy playing their instruments at the camp and gave concerts in the mess hall, sometimes attended by up to 2,000 people.

Austrian-born Ernst Kunwald, conductor of the Cincinnati Symphony Orchestra, was also interned. Kunwald, who once got into trouble for unapologetically expressing his sympathies for Germany and Austria before his orchestra performed the *Star Spangled Banner* at a concert, was arrested in December 1917 after a complaint from the Daughters of the American Revolution in Pittsburgh, urged the city's public safety director to ban a German from conducting the Cincinnati Symphony while on tour in Pittsburg. Kunwald's wife was also arrested. He resigned and was released a day later, but was arrested again the following month and put in an internment camp in Georgia. Kunwald was later deported and resumed his career in Europe in 1920. Kunwald and his makeshift orchestra practiced daily to help entertain the others in the camp, including the guards. They held concerts each Sunday at the camp's dining hall for local audiences of up to 2,000 people.

German music came under attack across the country. A Women's Society in Des Moines, Iowa, organized a boycott of a performance by the German opera star, Frida Hempel, in April 1918. The leaders of the boycott, many of the same people who had led the successful drive to eliminate German classes from all Des Moines public schools, issued a statement summing up their opposition: "We will not listen to music from a German when our boys are being killed and tortured."

In Omaha, Nebraska, orchestra conductor Otto Scharf was staying in the city's Nebraska Hotel. A group of zealous patriots agitating in the name of the Council of Defense began smearing yellow paint on the hotel. The hotel owner tried to stop the patriots, but they painted him yellow as well. Police arrested Scharf and charged him with disturbing the peace.

In Pittsburgh, the city council issued a city-wide ban on all music by Beethoven. The Metropolitan Opera Company of New York forbade the production of German works; the Philadelphia Orchestra said it would stop performing all German music, beginning November 10, 1917. The superintendent of schools in New Jersey announced that German music would be banned throughout the state. In California, the state board of education ordered that textbook pages containing German songs be cut out. "German music was the most dangerous form of German propaganda," the American Defense Society maintained, "because it appeals to the emotions and has power to sway an audience as nothing else can." Once-thriving German-language theaters in Milwaukee and St. Louis were also forced to close their doors during this late push to eradicate all things German. For some community theaters, their doors would stay closed forever.

Equally overwhelmed by the storm of patriotism in the spring 1918 were people who had simply spoken out to challenge the war effort. Under the broad powers of the Espionage and Sedition Acts, anyone claiming something as innocuous as "the draft is unconstitutional" could end up in jail. This targeted not only Germans, but also pacifists and leftists.

One of them was Eugene Debs, a union leader, an opponent of the United States' involvement in the war and America's best-known socialist at the time—thanks to his four presidential campaigns between 1904 and 1920. Debs, who descended from an Alsatian family, was convicted under the Espionage Act and sentenced to jail for ten years for making an antiwar speech. He was only released in 1921. Debs had stood up to then-President Grover Cleveland in 1894 and organized a strike of the railways workers, so he was already considered an enemy of the state.

Even more surprising was the conviction Robert Goldstein, a California businessman of German Jewish ancestry who supplied costumes to the emerging movie industry. He wanted to try making films and produced *The Spirit of '76* about the Revolutionary War. In the movie, which was released in May 1917 just one month after the United States entered the war, he depicted British redcoats shooting at women and children. This was said to be undermining the war effort because the United Kingdom was now an ally. He was charged in federal court of violating the Espionage Act by "aiding and abetting the German enemy." Goldstein received a ten-year prison sentence for the film, was released in 1921 after three years in jail and went to Germany for

15 years before he returned to the United States, this time fleeing the Nazis.

Also Wisconsin's famed Senator Robert La Follette, nicknamed "Fighting Bob," was also targeted. La Follette was in the Senate from 1906 to his death in 1926, and he steadfastly opposed any American involvement in the war. He criticized the United States' lack of neutrality before the war, arguing it was unfairly supporting Britain, France, and Russia by supplying munitions to the Allies but not giving Germany the same access, due to the shipping blockade. He only narrowly escaped censure by his colleagues at the Senate. Also, his own state legislature in Wisconsin tried—unsuccessfully—to censure him for his opposition to the war. The faculty of the University of Wisconsin, however, did vote to censure La Follette, as did the Wisconsin Teachers Association. Though he was later considered by historians to be one the best senators in U.S. history, La Follette, a tireless advocate of freedom of speech, was loathed in parts of the United States during World War I for his antiwar stance and his subsequent criticism of Wilson's handling of the war.

It seemed at times as if there were no limits to the drive to root out everything German in America. Those who saw themselves as patriots were not content with removing German from school classrooms, churches, newsstands, and concert halls. They wanted more. With organizational support from the American Defense Society, they turned their attention to having German books removed from public libraries as well. The Chicago Public Library took its entire German-language collection off its shelves. The Cincinnati Library hid all its German books from the public in storage rooms for the duration of the war and canceled all its subscriptions to German-language newspapers.

A Boy Scout leader in Flushing, Queens, signed a proclamation demanding that German language books be removed from public libraries in the city. "The whole trend of German argument and propaganda is dishonest, vicious, and criminal. This is true from the greatest philosophers down to the blatant soapbox pro-German orators. Their philosophy and even their theology are part and parcel of a carefully worked out campaign to uproot Christianity, to trample chivalry in the mud, to kill decency and to honor with gold lace, titles and money the pirate libertine, degenerate and murderer," the scout leader was quoted as saying in *The New York Times* on January 26, 1918.

Yet there may be no better illustration of America's hostility toward everything German than the spectacle of public book burnings. Ominous episodes of Americans setting German-language books on fire in public ceremonies across the country during World War I form a largely forgotten chapter in U.S. history, a skeleton in the closet of a country that would later scrutinize and condemn the Nazi book burnings that began after Hitler took power in Germany in 1933. American newspapers documented many ceremonial patriotic book burnings across the United States in the spring of 1918.

The American Defense Society especially urged Americans to burn German books and literature. Some of the book burnings were performed by mobs breaking into schools, searching for as many German-language textbooks as they could find, piling them on the ground outside, and setting them on fire. In other cities, it was not mobs who initiated the burnings, but administrators or officials. In Lima, Ohio, for instance, the board of education and city officials all participated in a book-burning ceremony. "In some communities indeed the superintendent of schools applied the fatal match," Carl Wittke wrote, noting that these demonstrations of patriotism often won warm approval from the local newspapers. "And the act was performed to the accompaniment of martial strains from the town band, patriotic songs by the children, and passionate oratory by their elders."

For a time, these book-burning ceremonies were all the rage in the United States—well-attended celebrations of patriotism. A book-burning ceremony was staged in Shawnee, Oklahoma, as part of the local Fourth of July celebrations. There was a book burning in Spartanburg, South Carolina, as well. In Colorado hundreds of people attended a German book-burning rally, and in Kansas enthusiastic patriots burned down a German private school. After

Columbus, Ohio, banned German instruction in local schools, the town filled with German immigrants went a step further by setting books on fire at a public book burning in the German Village quarter, at the foot of the Schiller statue on Broad Street.

In Davenport, Iowa, the Board of Education hosted a public book-burning ceremony in which students from several high schools set more than five hundred German textbooks on fire and sang patriotic songs as they stood watching the flames. The town's public library had also removed all of the German-language books from its shelves, deeming them "decidedly pro-German," according to the local newspaper, the *Davenport Democrat and Leader.* The newspaper praised the action as a "crusade to extract Kaiser Wilhelm's poisonous 'Kultur venom' from Iowa libraries." In Atlantic, Iowa, a mob stormed a high school and burned all of its German textbooks, shouting "No more German," on March 19, 1918.

In the town of Baraboo, Wisconsin, the Wisconsin National Guard started a bonfire of German books at a ceremony on Main Street on June 14, 1918. In Menominee, Wisconsin, when the school board issued an order forbidding the further instruction of German in the schools, it carried the hysteria a step further by ordering that all German textbooks in the city be "destroyed by fire" at a public gathering on June 7, 1918.

After the state's Council of Defense decreed a ban on the use of German in public and private schools, local residents of Butte, Montana, marked the start of their "War Chest" campaign to raise funds for the war effort by torching hundreds of German textbooks in a bonfire.

And in another Montana town, Fergus, where the local school board did not enact a German ban, a mob took the law into its own hands and stormed the school. About five hundred encircled the school while a group of mob leaders went in to collect the German textbooks. While the crowd sang the "Star-Spangled Banner" and set the books on fire, the principal was forced to publicly kiss the American flag to prove his loyalty to the United States. There was another fire in Fergus a few weeks later, when the school itself was burned down. Authorities were never able to determine who was responsible for that fire.

In Lewistown, Montana, local residents not only set fire to German books but they nearly lynched a suspected traitor at the same time as well, according to "Patriots on the Rampage: Mob Action in Lewistown 1917–18," an article by Anna Zellick in *Montana: The Magazine of Western History*. Zellick wrote, "Lewistown's citizens were quickly classified as either patriots or traitors. There seemed to be no middle ground, no place for calmness and common sense. Passive and silent loyalty was not acceptable. Irrationality and emotionalism increased in 1917–18, resulting in a mass hysteria that culminated in a public book-burning." Lewistown had a large immigrant population, she noted. "When war came, visible attachment to one's native country was suspicious to many American-born residents. Teaching young people the German language or anything about Germany came to be seen as support of 'the Kaiser.'"

"We are done with the days of a divided allegiance in this broad land of liberty," said local Lewistown leader Tom Stout at the town's inaugural Patriotic Day and Loyalty Parade on April 17, 1917. "With our sacred honor and the liberties at stake, there can be but two classes of American citizens, patriots and traitors! Choose you the banner beneath which you will stand in this hour of trial."

Even in towns that did not hold the book-burning ceremonies, German books disappeared from schools and libraries, quietly removed by local officials following government efforts to ban the teaching and speaking of German. Libraries in Detroit, Denver, St. Louis, New York, Cleveland, Portland, and Washington, D.C., all placed wartime bans on German books.

German culture in America was quickly disappearing in the United States, sometimes quietly, sometimes violently. Goethe and Schiller, Bach, Mozart, and Beethoven—their works either perished in the flames of public book burning ceremonies in America or were relegated to back shelves or basements during the dark World War I era.

*German-language books were frequently burned in public displays of
patriotism, sometimes after schools were raided to remove them.
Below: the remnants of a book burning in Baraboo, Wisconsin.*

Chapter 10

Tarred, Feathered, and Killed

The anti-German sentiment that swept the United States after the country entered the war in April 1917 forever changed America and attitudes toward its ethnic German minority. Accompanying the rush of patriotism was a rise in vigilante attacks against German-Americans. After the systematic campaign against on all areas of German culture in America, there was little left to attack but the people themselves.

Amid a surge of patriotism, many tens of thousands of Americans signed up to join the military even before President Woodrow Wilson introduced compulsory registration for the draft on May 10, 1917, for all men between the ages of twenty-one and thirty. Because there were so many German enclaves in the United States and because German-Americans had been active in keeping the country out of the war before 1917, patriots enthusiastic to do their part but ineligible for the draft had millions of German-speaking targets to choose from in their own backyards.

The German-Americans were one of the largest, most vibrant, and in some places among the loudest, most colorful, and at times even most obnoxious ethnic groups. As the war wore on, they also became America's most disliked, feared, and mistreated ethnic group. Frictions and tensions, which merely bubbled beneath the surface before 1917, erupted into open animosity and even wanton violence as the war progressed, exacerbated at times by the mercurial direction the war was taking with its uncertain outcome. The biggest wave of attacks coincided with the unexpected, albeit ephemeral, success of the German army's spring offensive in April 1918. As the hysteria against all things German surged during the first six months of 1918, at least thirty-five people were killed at the hands of mobs or in other violence that included several public hangings of Germans. In *Opponents of War: 1917–1918*, Horace Peterson and Gilbert Fite documented the killings and described the increase in public hangings and other mob-led murders as "patriotic affairs; they were murdering in the name of liberty and democracy."

Peterson and Fite also showed how the government chiseled away at freedom of speech, freedom of the press, and freedom of assembly with the Espionage and Sedition Acts. The 1917 and 1918 laws made it illegal to say or write anything that might even indirectly or remotely be seen as obstructing the war effort. Thousands were fined and sent to jail under the Espionage Act, which was first passed in April 1917 and then further strengthened with the Sedition Act in May 1918. A unique new form of "justice" spread across the nation, and reports of vigilantism—often heroically extolled—appeared with increasing frequency in the nation's newspapers.

One common form of warped justice meted out on German-Americans or German aliens suspected of being traitors was to tar and feather them—a painful form of public humiliation that had been used by mobs during the Colonial era to force their victims to conform. There was a wide variety of justifications cited for tarring and feathering people. Sometimes the mobs identified someone as a traitor, or sometimes they just singled out people with different opinions. "Tarring and feathering 'parties' were not uncommon and served as penalties for a multitude of offenses, ranging from failure to donate to the fund to buy uniforms for the Home Guards to expressions of disloyal and treasonable sentiments," noted historian Carl Wittke in *German-Americans and the World War*. "The victims were often seriously injured by the hot tar, and were otherwise humiliated and mistreated."

A tar-and-feather attack would usually begin with a group of people—that often quickly turned into a mob—forcing the victim to take his shirt off. Hot tar was poured or painted on the victim's back and chest, and he was forced to roll on a pile of feathers, which stuck to the tar. Mobs often paraded their victims through local streets and squares, with the aim of inflicting further humiliation and demanding that they either leave town or succumb to the mob's demands.

During World War I, incidents of tarring and feathering occurred in at least thirteen states, including Pennsylvania, California, Colorado, Ohio, Oregon, Mississippi, Kansas, Illinois, Iowa, Michigan, Nebraska, West Virginia, and Wisconsin, and in some cases resulted in fatalities.

In the spring of 1918, newspapers were filled with reports of tar-and-feathering attacks against Germans and German-Americans. E. A. Schimmel, a professor of modern languages in Ashland, Wisconsin, was suspected of being a German spy in April 1918. Members of the local Knights of Liberty, an aggressive group acting under the banner of patriotism, kidnapped Schimmel before tarring and feathering him. After the assault, an investigation found Schimmel was not a spy for Germany. But the mob got away with the kidnapping and assault, and there was no criminal investigation. Just a few weeks later, men wearing masks broke into the home of Adolph Anton, a bartender also of Ashland. Anton was taken outside his house, tarred, and feathered. On April 12, *The New York Times* reported that the bartender was attacked "because of his pro-Germanness."

In another tar-and-feathering incident, in Elk City, Oklahoma, on April 9, 1918, a preacher named William Madison Hicks, president of an organization called the World Peace League, was abused for a speech he had given nearly a year earlier in which he had allegedly said that "the men who are at the head of this war are nothing but a bunch of grafters and robbers. I would not register [for the draft] and I would not answer the call to the colors, and I do not believe anyone has to." Later, Hicks was convicted under the Espionage and Sedition Acts. He was sentenced to serve a twenty-year jail term in Leavenworth and fined $2,000. He spent five years in jail.

There was even at least one report of a woman being tarred and feathered. About sixty people dragged Harley Stafford of Montrose, Michigan, from her house during the night of April 12, 1918. The mob had broken into her home, bound and gagged her husband, and then took Stafford outside, where they tarred and feathered her. The mob accused her of having made disloyal remarks.

There were many horrid reports of attempts to kill Germans and German-Americans—in some cases for no apparent reason aside from the fact that the victim had a German name or spoke German. The reports of indiscriminate violence against Germans can be found in the pages of many American newspapers published in April and May 1918. For example, *The Cincinnati Volksblatt*, Ohio's most influential German-language daily, founded in 1835, reported on May 20, 1918, that a bartender in Hamilton, Ohio, was dragged from his saloon one night by a mob of about twenty-five men, all wearing masks. They accused him of failing to buy Liberty Bonds, tied a rope around him, and dragged him to a nearby canal before throwing him in. The man survived.

Police later said that, contrary to the vigilantes' accusations, the German-American bartender had bought Liberty Bonds and thrift stamps, securities issued by the government to help finance the war efforts. Government Liberty Bonds, issued to pay for the war, became a closely monitored barometer of a person's patriotism. Investor interest in World War I–era Liberty Bonds was only modest in some parts of the country, especially in the Midwest, where many pockets of Germans lived, which only raised further doubt about their loyalty.

Some of the campaign posters for Liberty Bonds included especially strong language and appeals to patriotism. "If you can't enlist, invest. Buy Liberty Bonds today," read one popular poster. Another poster alluded to earlier reports of atrocities in Belgium: "Must children die and mothers plead in vain? Buy Liberty Bonds," while yet another read, "Beat back the Hun with Liberty Bonds." There were many other reports of arbitrary violence against German-Americans during 1918. A

German farmer was shot in the back while working in his field near Hot Springs, Arkansas. He was shot, as the state's attorney later explained in defense of the assailant, because he had made "pro-German" statements. A German waiter was shot to death in Tulsa, Oklahoma, by an officer from the County Defense League for allegedly making "disloyal utterances." At the trial of Special Officer S. L. Miller, the defense attorney told the court about an unwritten law that made it justifiable for a person to kill another person who "speaks out against the country that shelters and nurtures him." Miller was found not guilty. Two days later, according to Peterson and Fite, the Tulsa County Council of Defense issued a proclamation stating, "Any person or persons who utter disloyal or unpatriotic statements do so at their own peril . . . and cannot expect the protection of the loyal citizenship of this nation."

Acts of violence against German-Americans took other forms as well. In Salt Lake City, a man named William Prisse was thrown into a dough bin by two coworkers after allegedly making "pro-German utterances." *The New York Times* reported that the fifty-one-year-old Prisse nearly suffocated when he was tossed head-first into the bin. The newspaper added that Prisse's two assailants also shot at his legs, which were sticking out of the bin.

There was an especially grisly case in San Jose, California, where a German-American tailor named H. Steinmetz was nearly killed by hanging. *The New York Times* published the following report on May 3, 1918:

Tarred and Feathered by the Knights of Liberty
New Organization in California to Stamp Out Disloyalty Finds Three Victims

"SAN JOSE, Cal., May 2.—H. Steinmetz, an Oakland tailor, was hanged here early today until he became unconscious; then he was tied to a tree, and later was taken away in an automobile by an organization known as the Knights of Liberty.

George Koelzer, who was tarred and feathered last night by members of the organization, was held in jail today for his own protection. Over the telephone today one of the 'Knights' said:

"'This organization has eighty-two members in San Jose and vicinity, with branches in San Francisco, Oakland, Stockton, Santa Rosa, Palo Alto and other places. We are going to stamp out disloyalty. We give a fair and impartial trial, and, if the evidence warrants, we turn the man over to the military or civil authorities.'

"Koelzer, a brewery worker, who was accused of pro-German activities, told the police that 'Knights of Liberty,' wearing black coats over their heads, took him from his room, carried him in an automobile five miles into the country last night, where they applied a coat of tar and feathers, and then brought him back to the city and chained him to a brass cannon in the city park, where he was found by the police.

"Richmond, Cal., May 2.—Guido Poenisch was taken from his home here last night by fifty white-robed persons, rushed to the municipal wharf, where he was 'tried' for disloyalty, and then tarred and feathered. He was 'found' not to have bought a Liberty bond and to have made disloyal remarks. Poenisch promised he would buy $100 worth of Liberty bonds and would join the Red Cross before his captors released him. He came here about ten years ago from Germany."

These were not the only incidents. Across the country, in Boston a rail worker was nearly killed by another mob. The Austrian-born employee of the Erie railroad stood accused by his coworkers of failing to show enough patriotism. They tied his feet with a rope and hoisted him upside-down about thirty feet above the ground, according to the *Boston Daily Advertiser* on May 7, 1918. The co-workers did not let him down and further ridiculed him while he dangled in the air. "A fire hose was played upon him. He was cut down an hour later by friends who found him alive," the newspaper reported.

There were other reports of violence against German-

Americans all over the country. Out west in Appleton, Colorado, the superintendent of schools, Dr. E. E. Cole, was forcibly taken from his home on April 12 by an armed mob that greased and feathered the distinguished educator. Cole was widely known and respected in teaching circles throughout Colorado, but that didn't matter to the vigilantes taking the law into their own hands. *The New York Times* reported that Cole was warned by the leader of the mob, who threatened, "If you don't leave town within the next thirty-six hours, we'll hang you to the nearest telephone pole." Cole was accused of stating that the German government had done more to advance the world's civilization in the five years before the war than any other nation. Cole denied making the statement. In another incident, in Los Angeles, a German boy was severely beaten because he refused to stand and sing "America."

There were several near-hangings of union leaders from the Industrial Workers of the World (IWW). A socialist union established in 1905, the IWW called for workers around the world to unite and for the abolition of capitalism. A disproportionately large number of German-Americans were members of the IWW. It was a powerful union at the time, notorious for initiating wartime strikes and engaging in disruptive activities. The large number of German-Americans in the IWW only served to further public doubts about their loyalties.

In Somerset, Pennsylvania, vigilantes tied a chain around the neck of traveling encyclopedia salesman Charles H. Kling and dunked him into a watering trough until he nearly drowned. The assailants accused Kling of blurting out in a local saloon that the Kaiser was "the best man in the world." Kling was grabbed by the other patrons in the saloon but managed to escape to his hotel room. A Red Cross meeting in the same hotel was just ending when the mob streamed into the hotel. The Red Cross members then joined the saloon patrons in raiding Kling's room. He was dragged outside, the heavy chain was placed around his neck, and he was led to the watering trough. "He was dunked several times, and forced to kiss the flag. Later, he was escorted out of town by a constable," according to the *Milwaukee Journal.*

In Pensacola, Florida, a German-American was flogged by a citizens group and forced to shout, "To hell with the Kaiser." The head of the Minnesota Safety Commission, John F. McGee, even called for the use of firing squads to wipe out "the disloyal element" in his state. Beyond the violence, German-Americans were often targets of harassment and sometimes viewed with suspicion merely for having a German name.

The Germanophobia in the United States during World War I was not merely aimed at one particular social class, nor did it take place in just a few isolated sections of the country. It was universal, cutting across all socioeconomic levels and geographical regions. Even President Wilson, who spent most of his first term working hard to keep the United States neutral and out of the war in Europe, turned against German-Americans and began speaking about "German spies" having infiltrated the nation.

On November 19, 1917, he issued a proclamation that barred all German males fourteen years and older from the vicinity of any place of military importance. Under the order, Germans were banned, for instance, from being within a half-mile radius of even the U.S. Forest Products Laboratory on the outskirts of Madison, Wisconsin. German aliens living in the United States were also barred from such places as Washington, D.C., the Panama Canal Zone, from all boats except public ferries, and from all airships, balloons, and airplanes. The 600,000 German aliens living in the United States at the time were required to register with local police, and were forbidden to relocate, the *Milwaukee Journal* reported on November 20, 1917. Thousands were interned as enemy aliens.

Zealotry was in no short supply, as private citizens and police officers sometimes reveled at the chance to display their patriotism under the new informal codes of justice. In New York, the prominent impressionist painter Childe Hassam was arrested for painting a steamship as it stood in the docks in the Hudson River. Police believed at first that they had captured a German spy. A few hours later, Hassam, whose family ties to the United States were found to be "as solidly American as the rocks of Plymouth," was soon released. He said he was not bothered by the incident and said it showed that New York City police were being alert, the *Milwaukee Journal* reported.

That most German-Americans were loyal to the United States and rallied behind the government as unreservedly as other American ethnic groups, especially after April 1917, did not seem to matter to many Americans who had already made up their minds about their German-American neighbors.

Fading memories: German-Americans marching in a present-day Steuben Parade in New York City, held in September.

Postscript

Lessons from the Past

The convulsions of anti-German sentiment that swept the country during World War I caused lasting damage. The German language, German books and newspapers, music, churches and communities, and even German-Americans themselves came under attack. And when the war ended and it was all over there was sadly little left. Where there was once a thriving German-language press in America, with hundreds of newspapers, only a handful survived. Where German was once taught in public schools across the nation, there was precious little of that left after 1918. Where German-American clubs and singing societies had once flourished, most were gone.

Prior to World War I, German immigrants had succeeded in keeping their language, culture, and traditions alive, an impressive bulwark against the forces of assimilation. But once the United States entered the war against Imperial Germany, German-American citizens, like Joseph Kirschbaum, introduced in the Dedication, got caught up in the middle the conflict and had little choice but to abandon their German language, traditions and culture.

"The extreme hysteria of the war period evaporated comparatively quickly, but a legacy of bitterness remained in America that is perhaps not even yet completely gone," John Hawgood wrote in 1940, in The Tragedy of German-America. When Hawgood returned to Belleville, Illinois, after World War I in 1929, he was astonished to find that the German influence had largely disappeared. "The German stock of Belleville was said to have no further connections with German culture," he wrote. "And immigrants from Germany arriving in recent years had little or nothing in common with them and did not appear to fit into the community." The Great War had stripped German-Americans of their Germanness. "Though the Germans, in America, as well as in Europe, emerged from the war unchastened and as fully convinced of the superiority of their own culture as ever, the German-Americans, as German-Americans, did not emerge at all," Hagwood continued. "The war had so enhanced the distance between the German and the American that no hyphen could stretch from one to the other. The German-Americans, disowned and derided by the Germans of Germany, had no further reason for clinging to their Deutschtum at such great sacrifices to themselves. It was perceived by all, at last, that German-Americanism was obsolete."

German culture and the sense of community was by and large wiped out by the end of World War I. According to the 2010 U.S. census, 49.8 million Americans considered themselves to be German-Americans, or sixteen percent of the total U.S. population of 309 million. This still tops the list of U.S. ethnic groups. Yet the census also revealed that just 1.7 percent of all Americans over the age of five spoke German even part of the time —in a country where more than ten percent of the population used German on a regular basis at the turn of the twentieth century.

Looking back to the years after the 9/11 terror attacks and the beginning of the Iraq war set against the backdrop of the World War I–era persecution of German-Americans, there are a number of uncanny parallels. It seems ridiculous today, but members of Congress actually changed the name of French fries to "Freedom fries" in their cafeterias, to punish the French for not following them into Iraq. The United States had been there before, in World War I, when a government agency decreed that sauerkraut should be called liberty cabbage and hamburgers be renamed liberty sandwiches. The changing of names in both eras was more than mere symbolism. It reflected a deeper antipathy. Pundits, late night comedy hosts, and sitcom writers alike denigrated the

French as "cheese eating surrender monkeys." The Germans were insulted for their reticence to fight in Iraq and called "weasels" in American papers such as *The New York Post*.

The fallout against Arab-Americans was, however, far worse. The ostracism, persecution, doubts about their loyalty, public humiliation, abuse, and indiscriminate physical attacks that German-Americans had been subjected to about ninety years earlier had eerie parallels with similar treatment endured by Arab-Americans and Muslims in general, and even by Sikhs, following the terrorist attacks of September 11, 2001. "When Americans have gone to war, it has historically been a religious experience," Professor Everett Long, a history professor at the University of Wisconsin–Whitewater, said. "The commitment to fight has had to either have been completely and zealously apparent or it has not been there at all." After the terrorist attacks on 9/11, innocent people in the United States once again became unwitting victims of out-of-control outbursts of "patriotic" behavior, as H.D.S. Greenway wrote in *The Boston Globe* in 2003.

When America entered World War I in 1917, German-Americans were hounded as the country succumbed to an anti-German hysteria that would have been unthinkable only a few months before. Looking back, we shake our heads and ask, 'how could it have happened? How could we have allowed these wrongs to have been carried out in our name?' Nowadays, these nightmares from the past seem as stupid and wrong as the Salem witch trials in 1620 when one Massachusetts community succumbed to fear and hysteria and sentenced nineteen people to be hanged for witchcraft and a twentieth to be pressed to death by heavy rocks. 'That could never happen today,' you say. Yet no one would have believed that people could be told to get up from airplane seats they had paid for and leave the aircraft for no other reason than someone on the flight felt uncomfortable having them aboard, usually because of a swarthy complexion. The United States is yielding to the fear of terrorism, and making huge mistakes that we will look back on one day with head-shaking amazement. Fear is a powerful motivator for repressive and cruel behavior.

Clemens Work, a journalism professor at the University of Montana, studied the attacks against Germans and the post-9/11 attacks and wrote a book called *Darkest Before Dawn: Sedition and Free Speech in the American West*, published in 2006. "The hair on the back of my neck stood up, the rhetoric was so similar, from the demonization of the enemy to saying 'either you're with us or against us' to the hasty passage of laws," he said.

Certainly there were considerable differences between the treatment of German-Americans during World War I and the treatment of Muslims after 9/11. To begin with, there was no dominant Muslim culture in America that could have been targeted. More importantly, the vigilantes did not escape unpunished. Rudy Giuliani, New York's mayor, ordered extra security for the city's mosques after 9/11, as did his successor, Michael Bloomberg.

However, there are similarities between some of the laws that were passed after 9/11 and those passed in 1917 and 1918 by state and federal legislatures. The Espionage Act of 1917 and the 1918 Sedition Act were designed to put limits on freedom of speech and freedom of the press, laws that scholars later called unconstitutional. The Espionage Act of 1917 made it a crime to try to stir up any kind of insubordination to the United States' war effort or to obstruct the recruitment or enlistment of volunteers to the army or navy. The Sedition Act of 1918 even made it a crime to express the wish that the war would end.

Likewise, the Patriot Act of 2001 gave authorities sweeping powers to detain immigrants indefinitely and also allowed police to search or wiretap a home or business without the owner's consent or even knowledge. The law gave authorities permission to search telephone, email, and banking records without judicial review. Arab-Americans and Muslims were fingerprinted, photographed, and subjected to questioning by authorities. They also suffered humiliating treatment in airports across the country. Some were indiscriminately removed from airplanes or not even allowed to board the planes, due to vague fears they could be terrorists. And so the rights of citizens were again limited in the name of patriotism.

The attacks on German-Americans and later Arab-Americans had a profound and lasting impact, leaving deep wounds and permanent scars on both. Nearly a century after patriotic Americans attacked German-Americans they had randomly assumed to be disloyal, another wave of intense patriotic fervor swept the country and enemies of the United States—whether real or perceived—were again vilified, ostracized and attacked.

"Those who cannot remember the past are condemned to repeat it"—eternal wisdom from George Santayana. A philosopher and novelist, Santayana was Harvard instructor who lived for long periods in both Europe and the United States. His words sound immortal but also resonate to anyone taking a closer look at the attacks on German-Americans. The notion that civil rights can—and will—be suspended or violated in times of war is still very much apparent, even in 2014, one hundred years after German-Americans were maltreated. In February 2014, U.S. Supreme Court Justice Antonin Scalia candidly told law students at the University of Hawaii that the Supreme Court's 1944 decision in the landmark case *Korematsu v. United States* was wrong when it ruled that the government was within its constitutional rights to put Japanese-Americans in internment camps during World War II. The Supreme Court in 1944 had upheld the convictions of Gordon Hirabayashi and Fred Korematsu for violating an order to report to an internment camp.

Scalia said the Supreme Court's 1944 decision came at a time when the United States was at war, and he cited a Latin expression—*inter arma enim silent leges* (in times of war, the laws fall silent)—as a sort of intellectual justification for America's violating the civil liberties of Japanese-American citizens. Scalia went even further, saying such violations of civil rights could well happen again. "Well of course *Korematsu* was wrong. And I think we . . . repudiated it in a later case. But you are kidding yourself if you think the same thing will not happen again. That's what happens.

It was wrong, but I would not be surprised to see it happen again, in time of war. It's not justification. But it is the reality."

Looking back at these chapters in American history got me thinking about the question: Could a better awareness of the crimes and injustices committed against German-Americans possibly have helped prevent what happened after 9/11? What if more Americans had been aware of that early twentieth-century history when the civil liberties and constitutional rights of German-Americans and German aliens were trampled upon with so little resistance? It's an intoxicating thought to consider that a greater awareness of past injustices might help prevent them from happening yet again.

These are questions that haunted me, and ultimately stirred me to take a new and deeper look at the subject that I first wrote about in my senior honors thesis as an undergraduate studying history at the University of Wisconsin. History indeed seemed to be repeating itself. A desire to try to shed further light on the abuses and humiliations that German-Americans endured during World War I compelled me to take a new look at the research I originally did in 1984, and to put it into a more comprehensive story for a wider audience in 2014. *Burning Beethoven*, marking the centenary of the beginning of World War I, is the result.

—Erik Kirschbaum, Berlin, August 2014

ERIK KIRSCHBAUM, a native of New York City, began learning German as a high school student and often wondered why it was hard to find anyone with whom he could practice speaking German. After studying German and history at the University of Wisconsin, he worked for newspapers in the United States before moving to West Germany in early 1989 to work as a foreign correspondent. He lives in Berlin. *Burning Beethoven* is his fourth book.

GERMAN LIFE IN AMERICA TODAY

BY HERBERT W. STUPP

The pre–World War I era of a thriving German culture in the United States is on occasion unearthed—quiet literally. In early 2014, when New York City construction workers dug deep into Manhattan to create a foundation for a towering new twenty-two-story hotel on the Bowery, they stumbled upon a treasure trove of German artifacts. Beer bottles, plates, beer mugs and other remnants of a once popular German tavern and theater called the "Atlantic Garden" were carried up to the light of day. The tavern was opened in 1858 by a German immigrant named Wilhelm Kramer, and for decades it was a hot spot for revelers before it closed in 1916 amid the anti-German hysteria that swept America during World War I.

New Yorkers and visitors frequented the "Atlantic Garden" to eat German food, drink German beer, watch plays, party, bowl, play billiards and listen to German folk music. The two-story building fell into disrepair in the decades that followed the closing, as the Bowery neighborhood also fell into disrepute. The building was gutted twice before it was finally demolished to make way for the new hotel. Its German heritage was long forgotten. Only in 2014, archaeologists excavated and preserved the artifacts—almost as if it were a prehistoric discovery unearthed in the midst of Manhattan. This saga is perhaps a partial metaphor for the state of German culture in America today.

A walk through major American cities will afford the stroller's ear many conversations in the languages of today's largest concentrations of new immigrants, speaking to each other in their native languages, such as Spanish, or Chinese. In New York City, the most recent conversations I've overheard in German were those of tourists. You don't often hear American citizens speaking German in New York—or almost anywhere else in the United States. Immigrant groups usually reach their peak influence in the U.S. in the most visible ways (such as restaurants, cultural clubs, and foreign language newspapers) when their maximum numbers of actual immigrants are present in the new homeland. That was certainly the case with German-Americans at the turn of the last century. But World War I changed all that.

But there are still traces of Germany in New York and in the United States today, and even new establishments that have opened up. There are fewer Turnvereine and Saengerbunds, and perhaps most obviously, there was a steady decline in the old German restaurants from the 1950s to the 1970s. High rents and perhaps a resistance to change, as far as the owners were concerned, doomed many of those old favorites. This includes institutions such as New York's famous Luchow's, Niederstein's, Kleine Konditorei and Café Geiger in the Yorkville neighborhood on the Upper East Side. Changing neighborhoods and the migration of the children of German immigrants to suburbs and to other states also shrank the customer base of the older restaurants.

American affinity and zeal for German products, however, seems to grow across various sectors, especially for cars. BMW, Mercedes, Porsche, Audi, and Volkswagen produce some of the finest vehicles on the market, and represent many Americans' "dream car." Consumers are often willing to spend more to purchase an appliance manufactured by Siemens, Bosch, and Miele because of their quality features and reliability. German beer is holding its own—and some brands, like Cologne-based Koelsch, has even made a recent appearance in the United States—and German wines like Riesling are doing well in America. The typical American with a VW in the driveway, Beck's beer and Selbach wine in the refrigerator, and Bosch appliances in the kitchen and basement, however, may be unaware that twenty, if not thirty percent of his American neighbors are of German extraction.

The "three German-American Steuben Parades continue to draw ten of thousands of people each autumn, ranging from the nation's largest Steuben Parade in New York City, down the famous Fifth Avenue, to proud, fun marches in Chicago and Philadelphia. The challenges of organizing a vibrant parade in a major city are not getting easier, yet a dedicated cadre of volunteers succeeds in making the New York parade on the third Saturday of September one of the most entertaining events in the German-American community, and in New York City.

Floats and music bands from the Tri-state area and from Germany entertain tens of thousands of visitors. The New York Steuben Parade has, in fact, grown during the last twenty years. In recent years, well-known New Yorkers like Ruth Westheimer —"Dr. Ruth"—have been Grand Marshals. And the post-parade Oktoberfest in Central Park is always a sold-out occasion. Some honored guests from Germany who attend the parade and related events have commented that they hear the German national anthem more often during the Steuben weekend in New York city than they do in an entire year in Germany.

Local operations of German airlines, car companies, importers and other services benefit from marketing their wares to attendees and marchers of the Steuben Parades. Their support is critical to the parades' ongoing success. And at the northern terminus of the New York Steuben Parade, at Fifth Avenue and 86th Street sits a magnificent mansion: The Neue Galerie, a museum exclusively devoted to displays of German and Austrian art, founded by former U. S. Ambassador to Austria Ronald Lauder. The museum opened in 2001 and is one of the finest vehicles presenting German culture to emerge in this century. Its reputation continues to grow, both with art critics and the general population. The Vienna-style café on the ground floor is equally popular.

But there is more: organizations like the American Council on Germany, the American Academy in Berlin, the German-American Hall of Fame, German-American Chambers of Commerce,

Cultural Vistas, Steuben Parade committees, and the German Heritage Museum present the contributions of Germans to the U.S., offer academic and other high-level exchanges, organize colorful Germanic celebrations, and provide other important links between America and the old country. Traditional organizations such as Chicago-based DANK and the Steuben Society (not directly affiliated with the Steuben Parades) remain active. So do Heimatvereine in St. Louis and other cities as well as regional dance and singing groups. But there are also newer organization that want to breathe new life into German culture in America, namely German Pulse, a web-based new enterprise based in Chicago, and Germany in New York, a local online guide for fun and events.

Speaking of fun: Across the nation, there are probably more local Oktoberfests organized today than ever before—in part a reflection of the large number of Americans of German heritage but also in part a tribute to the high level of respect and admiration most Americans have for things "Made in Germany." There are spirited events in far-flung places like tiny Hermann, Missouri, once founded by German winegrowers, and overlooking the Missouri river. More than a few of these festivals rely on Americans of various ethnicities for leadership, and they attract people of many backgrounds who enjoy the German-American food, music, beverages and culture, at least for a day. The Oktoberfest is becoming as American as the hamburger or the frankfurter!

Professor Don Heinrich Tolzmann, a retired historian who was curator of the German-Americana Collection, has done some research on German communities around the U.S. There are still various "German villages" that succeed in attracting tourists to visit, eat, stay and take out, especially during seasonal festivals such as Oktoberfest, Christmas and Rosenmontag. Such towns include Helen, Georgia; Leavenworth, Washington; Frankenmuth, Michigan; Hermann, Missouri; New Ulm, Minnesota; Oldenburg, Indiana, and two towns in Texas in the San Antonio area, New Braunfels and Fredericksburg.

These towns might be unknown to most Americans, but remain important outposts where people can savor a taste of German culture at will, some for the first time. Only several years ago, my wife and I attended a rollicking "Wurst Fest" in New Braunfels, Texas, where multiple German bands kept revelers waltzing and two-stepping day and night. Nearby in Fredericksburg, we ordered lunch from a German language menu in the town center, in one of many such restaurants. Fredericksburg also has a museum devoted to its German heritage.

Countering the disappearance of old restaurants is the emergence of new establishments that appeal especially to younger people. In New York City, master chef Kurt Gutenbrunner owns four German-Austrian restaurants, one of which is a Biergarten beneath the tourist-magnet High Line park overlooking the Hudson. Beer gardens and beer halls have opened in hipster Williamsburg, in Brooklyn and Astoria, Queens. In Manhattan, the Paulaner and Hofbrau breweries have opened their own restaurants featuring their products on tap. Hell's Kitchen has Hallo Berlin, Lederhosen in Greenwich Village serves Bavarian dishes in an informal setting.

The East Village has the Loreley pub, where customers can order Kölsch as well as Zum Schneider, with a huge selection of German beers as well as food (with a second location in Montauk). Across the street from Zum Schneider is Edie and the Wolf, an offshoot of the upscale uptown restaurant, Seasonal run by the same two chefs from Austria, Wolfgang Ban and Eduard Frauneder. Their restaurants have been featured on the *Today Show* and in *The New York Times*. Biergartens have also opened in center city Philadelphia and other major cities, including Seattle and Chicago. German restaurants serve customers in Alaska und Hawaii. Even Yuma, Arizona now features a popular German eatery, Das Bratwurst Haus, which opened in 2009.

Germans are having a major impact on America's retail food operations as well. The German discount supermarket chain Aldi now sports close to 1,500 supermarkets in the U.S., seven of them in New York City alone, and the popular Trader Joe's stores, also owned by the Aldi company, serve well over four hundred communities. And the regional powerhouse Waldbaum's supermarket chain is owned by the immigrant Haub family.

Twenty-first century America is also replete with leaders in nearly every sector of life who have Germanic roots. NFL football, golf, major league baseball, hockey, soccer and NBA basketball feature hundreds of players with German names. The latter includes a German immigrant, Dirk Nowitzki, who has been the NBA's Most Valuable Player. Jürgen Klinsmann, the former German soccer icon as a player, led the United States soccer team to a new level of success in the 2014 World Cup as head coach. At least five key U.S. team stars have German roots, including some playing in the Bundesliga today.

Business titans Donald Trump, the New York Stock Exchange's Duncan Niederauer, Microsoft founder Bill Gates Jr., the Steinbrenner family—the late George Steinbrenner was the owner of the New York Yankees—and Google chairman Eric Schmidt are all leaders in American enterprise today. Also a recent Nobel prize for medicine went to a German immigrant: Dr. Guenther Bloebel, who was born in Silesia, where his family had to flee after World War II, and studied in the German town of Tübingen.

Many Hollywood stars have Germanic roots, for instance, Sandra Bullock, Renée Zellweger, Kirsten Dunst, and Leonardo diCaprio were born to German immigrants, also Matt Groening, the creator of *The Simpsons*. And many younger Germans like to go to Hollywood to boost their careers, such as German-Austrian actor Christoph Waltz, and movie makers, directors and producers like Tom Tykwer, Wolfgang Petersen, Roland Emmerich, Katja Eichinger or Florian Henckel von Donnersmarck, the director of the Oscar-winning Stasi-drama *The Lives of Others*.

German-Americans are prominent in government as well: During the years that overlapped the presidencies of Bill Clinton and George W. Bush, all four leaders of America's federal legislative branch were of German descent. These men were Bill Frist, a Republican from Tennessee), majority and minority Leader, U.S. Senate; Tom Daschle, a Democrat from South Dakota, minority and majority Leader, U.S. Senate; Dennis Hastert, a Republican from Illinois, speaker, U.S. House of Representatives, and Richard Gephardt, a Democrat from Missouri, minority leader, U. S. House of Representatives. As I write, the Speaker of the House is German-American John Boehner, a Republican from Ohio, the state that used to be part of the so-called German triangle. And, of course, Brian Schweitzer, the former governor of Montana who pardoned German-Americans hanged in World War I posthumously, is of German descent.

The typical American or even German-American doesn't think of these accomplished people from an ethnic perspective. Today, they are simply Americans who are deserving of their fame, respect and recognition. And even eighty or one hundred years ago, it was often the same. Americans didn't think of baseball icon Babe Ruth, World War I–general General John J. Pershing, famed aviator Amelia Earhart or captain of industry Walter Chrysler as being German. They were fellow Americans.

Unless someone has an obvious accent, like Dr. Ruth Westheimer, supermodel Heidi Klum or Henry Kissinger, most people will focus first on a person's contributions, not their ethnicity. So, as to Germanic influence in the twenty-first century, it's complicated. Sadly, there are fewer people speaking German, taking Schuhplattler lessons and ordering sauerbraten in restaurants, but there are more people with Germanic roots reaching the highest echelons of American business, entertainment, academia, technology, journalism, government, military, sports, the arts, and other important sectors than ever before.

Our forebears, for the most part, would be pleased by this.

HERBERT W. STUPP, a native New Yorker, is a Trustee of the German-American Hall of Fame, an Executive Committee member of the German-American Steuben Parade, New York, and a member of the American Council on Germany. He has also been a New York City Commissioner, a federal official, a nonprofit CEO, and early in his career, an Emmy Award-winning editorialist at New York's Channel 9.

SOURCES AND CREDITS

Introduction

Bass, Frank. "U.S. Ethnic Mix Boasts German Accent Amid Surge of Hispanics." Bloomberg, New York, March 6, 2012.

Hawgood, John A. *The Tragedy of German America: The Germans in the United States of American During the Nineteenth Century–And After.* New York: Putnam, 1940.

Hickey, Donald. "The Prager Affair" in: *The Journal of Illinois State Historical Society.* Springfield, Illinois, 1969

Luebke, Frederick. *Bonds of Loyalty.* DeKalb, IL, Northern Illinois University Press, 1974.

Robbins, Jim, "Pardons Granted 88 Years After Crimes of Sedition." *The New York Times*, May 2, 2006.

United States Census 2010, U.S. Census Bureau.

Chapter 1

Hickey, Donald. "The Prager Affair," in *The Journal of Illinois State Historical Society.* Springfield, Illinois, 1969.

Luebke, Frederick. *Bonds of Loyalty.* DeKalb, IL: Northern Illinois University Press, 1974

O'Connor, Richard. *The German-Americans: An Informal History.* Boston: Little Brown & Co, 1968

St. Louis Globe-Democrat

The New York Times, April 20, 1914

Washington Post, April 12, 1914

Vought, Hans P. *The Bully Pulpit and the Melting Pot: American Presidents and the Immigrant, 1897–1933* Macon, Georgia: Mercer University Press, 2004.

The New York Times, April 20, 1914.

The New York Times, May 2, 2006.

Chapter 2

Hawgood, John A. *The Tragedy of German America: The Germans in the United States of American During the Nineteenth Century—and After*, New York: Putnam, 1940.

Fishman, Joshua A. *Language Loyalty in the United States: The Maintenance and Perpetuation of Non-English Mother Tongues by American Ethnic and Religious Groups*, The Hague: Mouton, 1966.

Luebke, Frederick. *Bonds of Loyalty*. Dekalb, Illinois: Northern Illinois University Press, 1974.

Mencken, Henry Louis. *The American Language*. New York: Alfred A. Knopf, 1919.

O'Connor, Richard. *The German-Americans: An Informal History*. Boston: Little Brown & Co, 1968

Kloss, Heinz. *The American Bilingual Tradition*. Rowley, Massachusetts: Newbury House Publishers, 1977.

Totten, Christine M. *Roots in the Rhineland, America's German Heritage in Three Hundred Years of Immigration 1683–1983*. New York: German Information Center, 1983.

Walter, Mack. *Germany and the Emigration 1816–1885*. Cambridge, Massachusetts: Harvard University Press, 1964.

Chapter 3

Hawgood, John A. *The Tragedy of German America: The Germans in the United States of American During the Nineteenth Century—and After*, New York: Putnam, 1940.

Luebke, Frederick. *Bonds of Loyalty*. Dekalb, Illinois: Northern Illinois University Press, 1974.

Moynihan, Daniel P., Nathan Glaze. *Beyond the Melting Pot*. Cambridge, Massachusetts: Massachusetts Institute of Technology Press, 1963

Wittke, Carl F., *German-Americans and the World War*, Columbus: Ohio State Archaeological and Historical Society, 1936.

The New York Times, April 5, 1918

Chapter 4

Allen, William C: *History of the United States Capitol: A Chronicle of Design,* Construction and Politics. Washington, D.C., 2001.

Bernhardi, Friedrich von. *Germany and the Next War.* New York: Longmans, Green, and Co., 1914.

Blum, Howard. Dark *Invasion 1915: Germany's Secret War and the Hunt for the First Terror Cell in America.* New York: HarperCollins, 2014.

Coben, Stanley. *A. Mitchell Palmer: Politician.* New York: Columbia University Press, 1963.

Doyle, Robert C. *The Enemy in Our Hands: America's Treatment of Prisoners of War from the Revolution to the War on Terror.* Lexington, Kentucky: University Press of Kentucky, 2010.

Hornady, William. *Awake America!* New York: Moffat, Yard & Co. 1918.

Hough, Emerson. *The Web: A Revelation of Patriotism: The Story of the American Protective League.* Chicago: Reilly & Lee, 1919.

Koenig, Robert. *The Fourth Horseman, One Man's Secret Campaign to Fight the Great War in America.* New York: Public Affairs Publisher, 2007.

Luebke, Frederick. *Bonds of Loyalty.* DeKalb, IL: Northern Illinois University Press, 1974.

Report on the Committee on Alleged German Atrocities. London: HMSO, 1915

Milwaukee Journal, April 14, 1918.

The New York Times, April 23, 1915, May 10, 1917, April 6, 1918.

The Nation, New York, 1918.

Painter, Jacqueline Burgin. *The German Invasion of Western North Carolina.* Ashville, North Carolina: Biltmore Press, 1992.

Sanders, M.L., and Philip Taylor. *British Propaganda During the First World War 1914–18.* London: Palgrave Macmillan, 1983.

Wilson, Trevor. "Lord Bryce's investigation into alleged German atrocities in Belgium, 1914-15." *Journal of Contemporary History,* London: Sage Publications, 1979.

Tuchman, Barbara W. *The Zimmermann Telegram.* New York: Macmillan, 1958.

Witcover, Jules. *Sabotage at Black Tom: Imperial Germany's Secret War in America 1914–17.* Chapel Hill, North Carolina: Algonquin Books of Chapel Hill, 1989.

Williams, Wythe. *Passed by the Censor: The Experience of an American Newspaper Man in France.* New York: E. P. Dutton, 1916.

Chapter 5

Roosevelt, Theodore. *The Foes of Our Household.* New York: George H. Doran Company, 1917.

Roosevelt, Theodore. *Fear God and Take Your Own Part.* New York: George H. Doran Company, 1916.

Skaggs, William. *The German-American Plot: German Conspiracies in America.* London: T. Fisher Unwin Ltd 1916.

Strother, French. *Fighting German Spies.* Garden City, New York: Doubleday Page, 1919.

North American Review. "Kill Spies." February 1918.

McClure's, July 1917, November 1917, April 1918.

The Nation, September 14, 1918.

Living Age, "The German Octopus", March 16, 1918.

Life, October 11, 1917, November 1, 1917.

Chapter 6

Hagedorn, Hermann. *The Menace of the German-Language Press.* The Outlook, August 15, 1917.

O'Connor, Richard. *The German-Americans: An Informal History.* Boston: Little Brown & Co, 1968.

Luebke, Frederick. *Bonds of Loyalty.* DeKalb, IL: Northern Illinois University Press, 1974.

Olds, Frank Perry. *The Atlantic Monthly,* July 1917.

School, John William. *America at War: A Handbook of Patriotic Education.* New York: National Security League, 1917.

Wittke, Carl. *The German-Language Press in America.* Lexington, Kentucky: University of Kentucky Press, 1957.

The Nation, June 8, 1918.

The Literary Digest, May 1918.

The Milwaukee Journal, October 15, 1915.

Philadelphia Inquirer, May 1918.

The New York Times, November 3, 1917.

Chapter 7

American Defense Society pamphlet. "Throw Out the German and All Disloyal Teachers," January 1918.

Benseler, David, Craig W. Nickisch, and Cora Lee Nollendorfs (editors). *Teaching of German in Twentieth-Century America*. Madison, Wisconsin: University of Wisconsin Press, 1983.

Hawgood, John A. *The Tragedy of German America: The Germans in the United States of American During the Nineteenth Century—and After*. New York: Putnam, 1940.

Curti, Merle and Vernon Carstensen. *The University of Wisconsin: A History 1848–1925*. Madison, Wisconsin: University of Wisconsin Press, 1949.

Fishman, Joshua A. *Language Loyalty in the United States: The Maintenance and Perpetuation of Non-English Mother Tongues by American Ethnic and Religious Groups*. The Hague: Mouton, 1966.

Grodzins, Morton. *The Loyal and the Disloyal*. Chicago: University of Chicago Press, 1956.

Hagedorn, Hermann. *Where Do You Stand? An Appeal to Americans of German Origin*, New York: Macmillan, 1918

Hohlfeld, Alexander Rudolph. *The Wisconsin Project on Anglo-German Literary Relations*. Madison, Wisconsin: University of Wisconsin Press, 1949.

Luebke, Frederick. *Bonds of Loyalty*. DeKalb, IL: Northern Illinois University Press, 1974.

Mencken, Henry Louis. *The American Language*, New York: Alfred A. Knopf, 1919.

Meyer, Ernst E., *Hey Yellowbacks! The War Diary of a Conscientious Objector*, New York: Literary Licensing, 1930.

Mollenhoff, Dave, Madison: *A History of the Formative Years*. Madison, Wisconsin: University of Wisconsin Press, 1982.

O'Connor, Richard. *The German-Americans: An Informal History*. Boston: Little Brown & Co, 1968

Peterson, Horace and Gilbert Fite. *Opponents of War: 1917–18*. Madison, Wisconsin: The University of Wisconsin Press, 1986.

Wittke, Carl F. *German-Americans and the World War*. Columbus, Ohio: Ohio State Archaeology and Historical Society, 1936.

The New York Times, February 3, 1918; March 18, 1918; April 5, 1918; April 11, 1918.

School Life, U.S. Office of Education, August–December.

The Journal of Education, January 31, 1918; February 17, 1918; April 25, 1918; July 18, 1918; October 17, 1918; November 7, 1918.

School and Society, June 1, 1918; June 8, 1918.

Milwaukee Journal, April 9, 1918; April 10, 1918; April 11, 1918; April 14, 1918; April 21, 1918.

Wisconsin Journal of Education, December 1917.

The Nation, November 19, 1918; March 30, 1918.

The New Republic, 1918.

The Literary Digest, April 20, 1918.

Chapter 8

Hawgood, John A. *The Tragedy of German America: The Germans in the United States of American During the Nineteenth Century—and After.* New York: Putnam, 1940.

Hornady, William. *Awake America!* New York: Moffat, Yard & Co, 1918.

Hough, Emerson. *The Web: A Revelation of Patriotism: The Story of the American Protective League.* Chicago: Reilly & Lee, 1919.

Luebke, Frederick. *Bonds of Loyalty.* DeKalb, IL: Northern Illinois University Press, 1974.

Wittke, Carl F. *German-Americans and the World War.* Columbus, Ohio: Ohio State Archaeological and Historical Society, 1936.

Chapter 9

Garraty, John Arthur. *The American Nation: History of the United States Since 1865.* New York: Longman, 1997.

Hawgood, John A. *The Tragedy of German America: The Germans in the United States of American During the Nineteenth Century—and After.* New York: Putnam, 1940.

Hornady, William. *Awake America!* New York: Moffat, Yard & Co, 1918.

Hough, Emerson. *The Web: A Revelation of Patriotism: The Story of the American Protective League.* Chicago: Reilly & Lee, 1919.

Luebke, Frederick, *Bonds of Loyalty,* Dekalb, Illinois: Northern Illinois University Press, 1974.

Pifer, Richard L. *Total War on the Home Front: La Crosse, Wisconsin and the World War,* Madison, Wisconsin: University of Wisconsin Press, 1976.

Peterson, Horace and Gilbert Fite: *Opponents of War: 1917–18.* Madison, Wisconsin: University of Wisconsin Press, 1986.

Wittke, Carl F. *German-Americans and the World War.* Columbus: Ohio State Archaeological and Historical Society, 1936.

The New York Times, January 26, 1918.

Chapter 10

Garraty, John Arthur. *The American Nation: History of the United States Since 1865.* New York: Longman, 1997.

Hawgood, John A., *The Tragedy of German America: The Germans in the United States of American During the Nineteenth Century—and After.* New York: Putnam, 1940

Luebke, Frederick. *Bonds of Loyalty.* DeKalb, IL: Northern Illinois University Press, 1974.

Peterson, Horace and Fite, Gilbert. *Opponents of War: 1917–18.* Madison, Wisconsin: University of Wisconsin Press, 1986.

Wittke, Carl F.. *German-Americans and the World War.* Columbus: Ohio State Archaeological and Historical Society, 1936.

The New York Times April 9, 1918; April 13, 1918; May 3, 1918.

The Cincinnati Volksblatt, May 20, 1918.

The Boston Daily Advertiser, May 7, 1918.

Milwaukee Journal, November 20, 1917; April 11, 1918; April 21, 1918.

The Literary Digest, May 1918.

The Nation, July 6, 1918.

The Commoner. Lincoln, Nebraska. September 6, 1918

Picture Credits:
Front Cover: Wisconsin Historical Society
Pictures pp. 70, 73, 74: National Archives
Pictures pp. 14, 27, 30, 35, 148: Eva C. Schweitzer
Pictures p. 138: Wisconsin Historical Society
Pictures pp. 50, 56, 100, 118: Postcard/Propaganda Poster
Pictures pp. 24, 46, 61, 86: Life
Back Cover: Galip Ölmez

Berlinica presents

2010–2015 Program

Welcome to Berlinica, the first American publishing company devoted to Berlin! If you subscribe to our monthly newsletter at

http://www.berlinica.com/contact.html

You will get one of those two e-books below for free. All you need to do is go to our website and sign up.

New Berlinica books in 2015

Sebastian Ringel

LEIPZIG!

ONE THOUSAND YEARS
OF GERMAN HISTORY
BACH, LUTHER, AND FAUST:
THE CITY OF BOOKS AND MUSIC

Softcover, 224 pp., full color, $25.95
ISBN: 978-1-935902-58-1

"Humerous and tragic stories
from 1000 years of Leipzig"

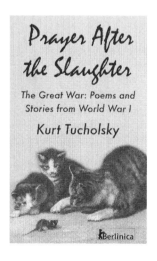

Kurt Tucholsky

PRAYER AFTER THE SLAUGHTER

POEMS FROM WORLD WAR I

Bilingual Edition, translated by
Peter Appelbaum and James Scott

Softcover, 116 pp., 6 bw pictures,
$12.95, ISBN: 978-1-935902-28-7

"He heaped scorn on the reaction-
ary institutions of the old regime"

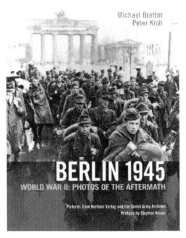

Michael Brettin / Peter Kroh

BERLIN 1945

WORLD WAR II:

PHOTOS OF THE AFTERMATH

From the Soviet Army Archives

With a Preface by Steven Kinzer

Softcover, 218 pp., 177 bw pictures
$25.95, ISBN: 978-1-935902-02-7

"Even if you think you've seen it all, Berlin 1945 will surprise you"

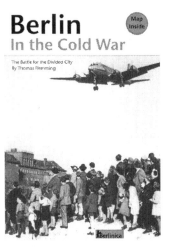

Thomas Flemming

BERLIN IN THE COLD WAR – THE BATTLE FOR THE DIVIDED CITY

Softcover, 90 pp., $11.95
51 bw pictures, 3 maps
ISBN: 978-1-935902-80-5

"The story of the divided city in a nutshell, without missing a beat"

Michael Cramer

THE BERLIN WALL TODAY

REMNANTS, RUINS REMEMBRANCES

Softcover, 100 pp., $15.95
Full color, 150 pictures,
ISBN: 978-1-935902-10-2

"A well-illustrated book"

Erik Kirschbaum

ROCKING THE WALL

BRUCE SPRINGSTEEN:
THE BERLIN CONCERT THAT CHANGED THE WORLD

Softcover, 168 pp., 45 color pictures, $16.95, ISBN: 978-1-935902-82-9

"A statement of the power of music as anyone, ever, has come up with"

Andreas Austilat

MARK TWAIN IN BERLIN

NEWLY DISCOVERED STORIES & AN ACCOUNT OF TWAIN'S BERLIN ADVENTURES
Preface by Lewis Lapham

Softcover, 176 pp., 67 bw pictures, $13.95, ISBN: 978-1-935902-95-9

"This fascinating book is a must-read for any Twain enthusiast"

Holly-Jane Rahlens

WALLFLOWER

A BERLIN NOVEL

Softcover, 146 pp., $12.95
ISBN: 978-1-935902-70-6

". . . an absorbing story of two people who are trying to figure out who they are and a fascinating look at the dawning of a new era in Germany . . ."

Andreas Nachama
Julius Schoeps
Hermann Simon

JEWS IN BERLIN

Preface by Carol Kahn-Strauss

Softcover, 314 pp., $25.95
376 pictures, color & b/w
ISBN: 978-1-935902-60-7

"... a captivating read that promises a wealth of enjoyment ..."

Kurt Tucholsky

BERLIN! BERLIN!

DISPATCHES FROM THE WEIMAR REPUBLIC

Preface by Anne Nelson
Introduction by Ian King

Softcover, 198 pp., 41 pictures, $13.95
ISBN: 978-1-935902-23-2

"... the most brilliant, prolific, and witty cultural journalist of his time"

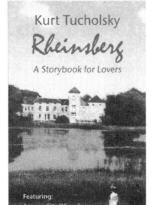

Kurt Tucholsky

RHEINSBERG

A STORYBOOK FOR LOVERS

WITH: AMONG CITY WIZARDS
Afterword by Peter Boethig

Hardcover, 96 pp., 35 pictures, $14.95
ISBN: 978-1-935902-25-6

"This book was the blueprint for love for an entire Generation"

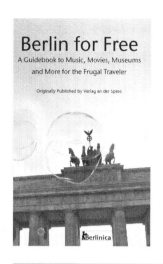

Monika Maertens

BERLIN FOR FREE

A GUIDEBOOK TO MOVIES, MUSEUMS, MUSIC, AND MORE FOR THE FRUGAL TRAVELER

Softcover, 104 pp., $11.95
ISBN: 978-1-935902-40-9

"This book is an investment that pays for itself—whoever wants, or has to save, needs it"

Lothar Heinke

WINGS OF DESIRE ANGELS OF BERLIN

Softcover, 102 pp., $19.95
123 full color pictures
ISBN: 978-1-935902-18-8

"A book full of anecdotes about the angels throughout the city – and a search for angelic traces"

Rose Marie Donhauser

THE BERLIN COOKBOOK

TRADITIONAL RECIPES AND NOURISHING STORIES

Hardcover, 104 pp., $21.95
61 recipes, 98 color pictures
ISBN: 978-1-935902-51-5

"Beautiful pictures, entertaining texts, and easy to process, fresh ingredients"

Adrienne Haan

BERLIN – MON AMOUR

A TRIBUTE TO 1920S GERMANY IN MUSIC

Music CD, 50 minutes
In English or German
$ 15.95, only on Amazon

"Grace, elegance, power"

Rosemarie Reed

THE PATH TO NUCLEAR FISSION

NARRATED BY LINDA HUNT

Movie DVD, run time 81 min
German / English, subtitled
$19.95, only on Amazon

"... honors the lives of women who were more than significant ..."

Stefan Roloff

THE RED ORCHESTRA

A DOCUMENTARY ABOUT THE GERMAN ANTI-NAZI RESISTANCE

Movie DVD, run time 57 min.
German and English, subtitled
$24.95, only on Amazon

". . . danger invaded normalcy . . . landscape threatens to tumble . . ."

Made in the USA
San Bernardino, CA
26 September 2015